How to produce better worksheets

Robin Lloyd-Jones

Stanley Thornes (Publishers) Ltd

First published in 1985 by Hutchinson Education
Reprinted in 1988

Reprinted in 1990 by:
Stanley Thornes (Publishers) Ltd
Ellenborough House
Wellington Street
CHELTENHAM
Glos. GL50 1YD. England

British Library Cataloguing in Publication Data

Lloyd-Jones, Robin
How to produce better worksheets.
1. Work sheets (Education)—Great Britain
I. Title
371.3'07'8 LB1043.2.G7

ISBN 0 7487 0344 6

Printed and bound in Great Britain
Reprinted 1994, 1995 (twice)

Contents

Acknowledgements

Thanks are due to the following for permission to reproduce copyright material.

Table 3: Taken, with permission, from *Arrangements in Standard Grade Science at Foundation and General Levels*, Scottish Examination Board

Table 7: Taken, with permission, from *Standard Grade Mathematics at Foundation, General and Credit Levels*, Scottish Examination Board

Case Study 5: Taken from *Reading for Understanding*, Junior Edition, Thelma Gwinn Thurstone. Copyright 1963 Science Research Associates, Inc. All rights reserved. Reproduced with the permission of the publisher.

Extract C: Illustration Calum Campbell

Figure 39: The Glasgow Geography Panel S1/S11 Working Party, 1976–79

Case Study 14: Janet Jenkins, *How to write a distance learning course*, Unit 6: Planning for writing, C.E.T.

Table 13: Bruce Gillham, *How to write a distance learning course*, Unit 11: Setting up an evaluation, C.E.T.

Example 14: *How to write a distance learning course*, Unit 8: Editing and production, C.E.T., copyright Open University

Example 20: P. Ashton, P. Hunt, S. Jones, G. Watson, *Curriculum in action: An approach to evaluation* (Course Number P234), Open University (1980)

Figures 66–8: Reproduced with the permission of Her Majesty's Stationery Office

Table 12: I. N. McPherson, *Evaluation in Education Unit 1*, Learning Resources Unit, Dundee College of Education

Example 26: Reprinted by permission of William Heinemann Limited

Preface

This is a time of curriculum change. Teachers are being given more and more responsibility for devising the learning materials which are needed to respond to new syllabuses, new teaching methods and new modes of assessment. Much of this new material will be in the form of worksheets.

This book does not attempt to convert you to using worksheets. I start with the assumption that you already use them, are well aware of the advantages of doing so and would like to produce the most effective worksheets possible in the time available to you. I have tried to offer practical suggestions on ways of doing this.

R L-J

To my former colleagues
at Dunbartonshire's
Curriculum Development Centre

Chapter One

The wood and the trees

In more than a decade of evaluating worksheets, advising working parties and running workshops for teachers in the production of worksheets, my experience has been that there are seven main faults to be found in worksheets:

- They do not cater for the full range of ability in the classroom.
- The language they use is too difficult.
- The visual quality and layout is poor.
- There is insufficient variety of stimulus.
- There is lack of clarity about objectives.
- There is mindless filling of blanks, and not enough processing of information.
- It is not possible to see the wood for the trees.

Not catering for the full range of ability

Even when classes are not organized on a mixed-ability basis, there can be surprisingly large ranges of ability and of speeds of working. Does your material provide for the needs of the slow learner and the fast learner? How do you discover who is having difficulties and what remedial action do your take? Chapter 3 takes a closer look at some possible answers to these questions.

Using language which is too difficult

This, of course, is allied to the first point. Many worksheets use a vocabulary and sentence structure which is too difficult for the less able members of a group. Chapters 6 and 7 discuss these matters more fully.

Poor visual quality and layout

This may be typified by a sheet of unrelieved text (often in poor handwriting). Most pupils are more motivated by the appearance of a worksheet than by its contents. You do not have to be an artist or a graphic designer to improve the visual quality of a worksheet. Chapter 9 discusses ways of doing this which are within the capabilities of any teacher.

Insufficient variety

Children learn in different ways. They therefore need a variety of stimuli and need to be able to respond in a variety of ways, e.g. through writing, talking, drawing, mime, modelling, observing. There is the obvious point, too, that material lacking in variety is just plain dull. Variety of approach is implied and exemplified throughout the book, but here is a brief checklist.

Variety of location
In writing worksheets you are constructing learning situations and some of these situations should involve locations other than the desk where the pupil sits – e.g. class, school or local library, maps and charts displayed on the wall, the environment around the school, worksheets associated with field studies, and visits to places outside the school walls.

Variety of resources
Do you use a variety of resources, or are your worksheets completely self-contained? Are your worksheets sometimes used in conjunction with the blackboard, the OHP, slides, film, video? Do they make references to visits or speakers?

Do your worksheets make reference to textbooks? If not, what opportunities are you providing for your pupils to handle books and look up information for themselves? Are you satisfied that the visual quality of your material matches up to what textbooks and the commercially printed media can provide?

Variety of learning situations
How many of the learning situations listed below have you included?

Learning situations	
Exposition Demonstration	teacher → student
Text Audio-visual media	resource → student
Discussion Case study Seminar	teacher ↔ student
Role playing Debate Simulation	student ↔ student
Practical work Document handling Programmed instruction	student ↔ resource

What opportunities have you provided for group work (groups by interest, by ability, by mixed-ability, by sex, random groups)?

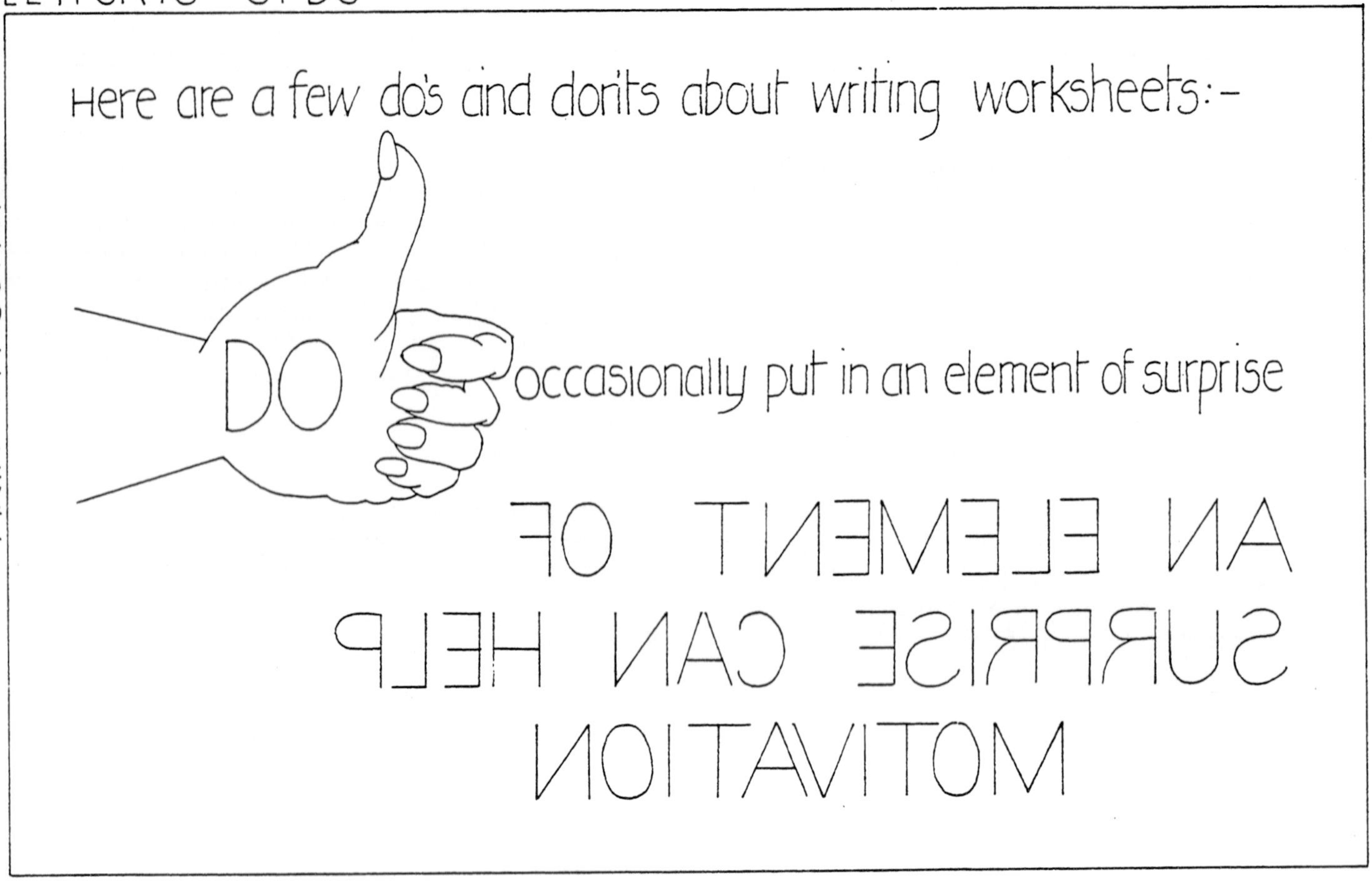

Here are a few do's and don'ts about writing worksheets:-

DO occasionally put in an element of surprise

AN ELEMENT OF SURPRISE CAN HELP MOTIVATION

DON'T invite your pupils to play the game called, 'GUESS WHAT'S IN THE TEACHER'S MIND'.

IN THE MIDDLE EAST JEWS LIVE IN..............?

Tents? Poverty? Cities? Discomfort? Fear of the Arabs?

Variety of activity
Is there a variety of choice? At certain points, do you offer a choice of activities? Is there a balance between open and closed questions? At one end of the continuum a closed question has only one correct answer; at the other end, an open question has a minimum limitation on content, structure or style and the answer is a matter of opinion and judgement.

Lack of clarity about objectives

Allied to a consideration of variety is the range and variety of objectives which worksheets attempt or do not attempt to meet. More than once I have been shown courses which have impressive-looking objectives which are stated in the introduction, but not reflected in the actual worksheets. We tend, often unconsciously, to emphasize those objectives which are easily taught or easily assessed. Do your worksheets, in fact, teach your course objectives? Do you know what the course objectives are? Are you sure that these are the most worthwhile and useful objectives for your pupils to attain?

Do you attempt objectives which are not appropriate to worksheets? Do your worksheets reflect a good range and balance of higher and lower order objectives, or do they tend to emphasize knowledge and understanding at the expense of everything else?

Do your pupils know what these objectives are? Your younger pupils do not have an overview, like you do, of where the course is heading; of what is important and what is not; which facts and skills are of long-term use and which are only of immediate use. All new knowledge is likely to be given equal emphasis unless you provide some guide or map of where they are heading and why.

What learning experiences can you devise through your worksheets that will help pupils to achieve the course objectives? In what ways can worksheets help diagnose the problems which pupils are having in trying to meet these objectives?

What part can worksheets play in assessing whether your objectives have been attained?

Chapter 5 looks more closely at these matters and at the role of worksheets in a criterion-referenced system.

Failure to process information

Case study 1

This is a simple demonstration of how a worksheet can be structured so that the information is processed by the user.

In Figure 1(a) the information is not processed. In Figure 1(b) more processing takes place because the response does not exactly match the information and therefore thought is required before an answer can be given.

> The *nucleus* is the centre of the atom.
> Round it orbit the *electrons*.
>
> The ________ is the centre of the atom.
> Round it orbit the ________.

> The *nucleus* is the centre of the atom.
> Round it orbit the *electrons*.
>
> The ________ orbit round the ________.

Figure 1(a) and (b) *Case study 1*

In Figure 2 the learner has to interpret the diagram and process visual information into the form of a sentence.

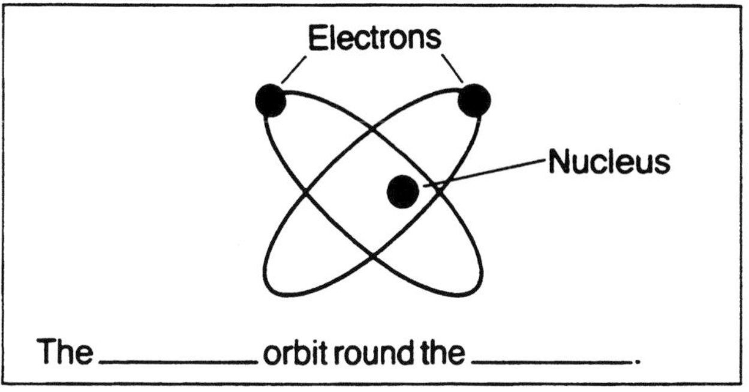

Figure 2 *Case study 1 – introduction of a diagram and more processing of information*

But *beware!* In Figure 3 what purpose does the diagram now serve? Can the pupil answer the question without looking at the diagram?

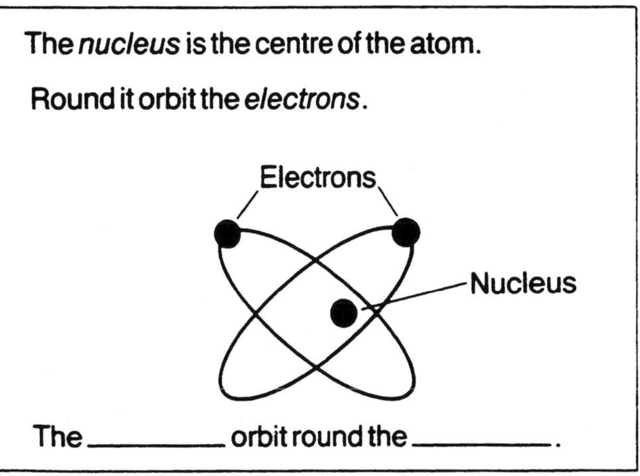

Figure 3 *Case study 1 – does the diagram serve a purpose?*

Pictures are useful if they illustrate a point. If used indiscriminately, they lose their effect.

In these examples, the teaching point was the specific words 'nucleus' and 'electrons'. In other types of worksheets the processing of information can be done by asking pupils to generate their own language rather than reproduce the words already supplied.

Not seeing the wood for the trees

This is not a 'theoretical' book, but every classroom activity has a theoretical background. Even the simple instruction 'Get out your books' assumes theories of worthwhile knowledge, of how pupils learn, of what the aims of education are and the best ways of achieving them. Similarly, every worksheet says something about your relationship with your pupils, about how you feel about them on a personal level, about what you think they should learn and how they should learn it. It is all too easy to plunge into production without first standing back and 'seeing the wood' as a whole.

What assumptions are you making about the overall purposes of education and of your subject? About the needs of the pupils? Is the material you are producing worthwhile? What criteria do you use to judge worthiness? Is the material better than what it is replacing? What is your definition of better?

Table 1

From	*To*
Classes treated as one homogeneous unit.	Recognition of individual differences.
Emphasis on content and didactic methods.	Emphasis on process and concepts and self-discovery methods.
2 × 4 teaching. (Two covers of the textbook, four walls of the classroom).	Multi-media materials, practical and oral work, links with the community.
Teacher as instructor in a role of authority.	Teacher as manager of resources and learning experiences.
Emphasis on factual knowledge and academic studies.	Increasing emphasis on social, emotional, moral and aesthetic development.
Transmission of past culture.	Transformation of present and future society.
Learning experiences determined by the requirements of the subject.	Learning experiences determined by individual needs, interests and viewpoint.

What is your rationale for the decisions you have made concerning where you want to place your material in relation to Table 1? What degree of teacher control is implied in your material? What teaching methods and types of classroom organization are assumed? What policy regarding the deployment of resources are you using - open access, controlled access, limited access? (See Chapter 4.)

Much teaching, especially in subjects like English or the Social subjects, concerns specific value positions. Are you aware that values are being put across by your material? Are such values assumed or implied without actually being stated? Are they mentioned without comment? Are they put up for discussion?

Worksheets are a tangible expression of your aims, of your interpretation of the syllabus, of your feelings about the subject, of your general view of what teaching and learning are about. So it is not an airy-fairy waste of time to stand back and ask yourself these fundamental questions.

I shall end this introductory chapter by stating two final points which are aspects of seeing things in a wider perspective. First, the construction of worksheets should not be a lone activity - two heads are better than one and pooled judgements are more valid. Second, worksheets are not the answer to every learning situation - always consider the alternatives. No course should be 'death by a thousand worksheets'.

Chapter Two

The worm in your worksheet

This chapter analyses how and why a particular worksheet changed during its evolution. Although the worksheet we look at is taken from a Science course, the points and principles arising out of this study apply to worksheet construction in general and have relevance for all teachers.

Case study 2
The case study is based on a study written by Katherine Menmuir, Dundee College of Education Learning Resources Unit, *Testing your Material: Field Testing* (1983). It concerns a worksheet with the title 'Looking at worms', which is part of the Scottish Integrated Science Course for the first two years of secondary school (in Scotland, secondary education starts at the age of twelve). The material was prepared by a working party of the Scottish Central Committee on Science and was field tested in many schools from 1974 to 1977.

On the basis of comments from the teachers who tried out the material, this worksheet underwent three main rewrites. Versions A, B and C (Figures 4–6, pp. 10–12) show the changes which were made. Version D (Figure 7, p. 13) is the final worksheet published by Heinemann.

The worksheets were accompanied by a Teachers' Guide from which the following extract comes:

Expected outcomes: Ability to:
- make observations;
- draw conclusions from observations;
- communicate.

The main intention underlying CS1 is the development of the pupils' ability to observe phenomena and draw conclusions based on these observations. A study of characteristics, movement and reaction to stimuli of the worm is used as a vehicle whereby these intentions may be realized.

Although most of the examples and case studies in the following chapters are individual worksheets, we must remember that a worksheet does not stand alone. It can only be fully evaluated within:

- the course as a whole and the overall balance of the component parts of that course;
- the context in which it is used and the general framework of explanation and support that surrounds it.

The level of difficulty, for example, cannot be discussed without knowing whether the teacher first went through the worksheet orally.

Differences between version A and version B
There is a basic change in layout. In version A, it is not at all clear in what order you look at the squares, the vertical and horizontal lines being equally dominant. In version B, the numbering of the horizontal layout indicates clearly how you should tackle the work. The horizontal division of each section gives more flexibility to the layout, particularly where diagrams are concerned.

Version B has been given a heading in larger and heavier lettering.

The amount of pupil activity has increased from A to B as shown in Table 2. In particular, the activity about comparing shapes does not appear on version B. This was rather a pointless activity, particularly as a worm is a changing, not a fixed, shape.

Table 2

Type of Activity	*Worksheet A*	*Worksheet B*
Practical Activity	7	18
Written Responses	5	5
Mental Responses	2	8

Too many questions in version A could be answered simply by 'yes' or 'no'. Version B comes nearer to the stated objectives of making observations and communicating them.

Differences between version B and version C
In version B, when a question is asked, it is not always clear whether a written or a mental response is required. Version C remedies this by:

- turning the question into the implied instruction, e.g. 'Can you see the short hair?' becomes 'Look for the short hair';
- putting in unfilled lines where a written answer is required. However, in version C, section (c), is that line for a written answer, or is it a dividing line between two activities?

In B2 the shape of the answer box leaves it open to doubt as to whether it should be filled by a drawing or by a word. C(c) substitutes a blank line for a box, making it clear that a word is expected.

There are three main changes between B3 and its counterpart C(c):

- In B2 the arrangement of different type styles, underlines and the box were confusing, so this has been remedied.

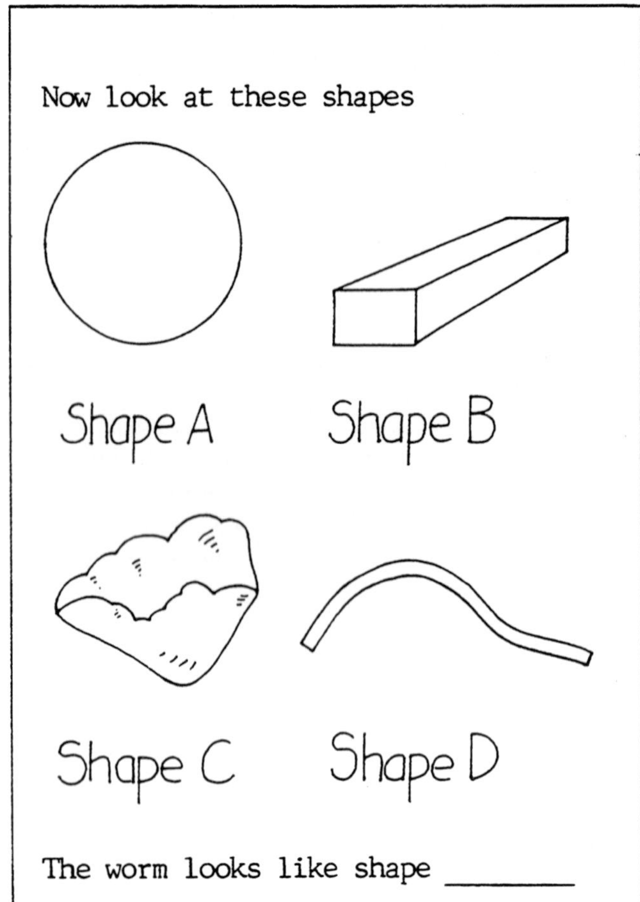

Now look at these shapes
Shape A
Shape B
Shape C
Shape D
The worm looks like shape ______

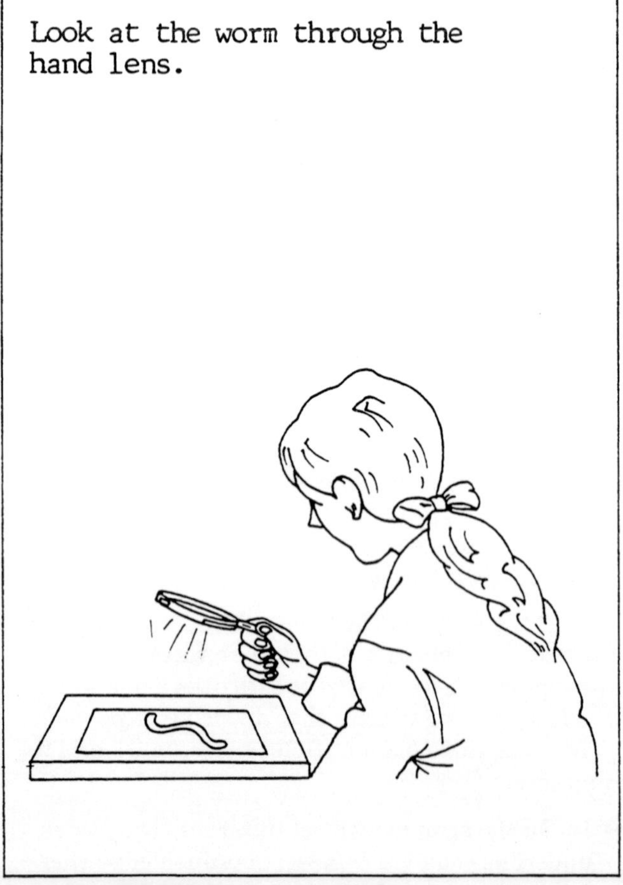

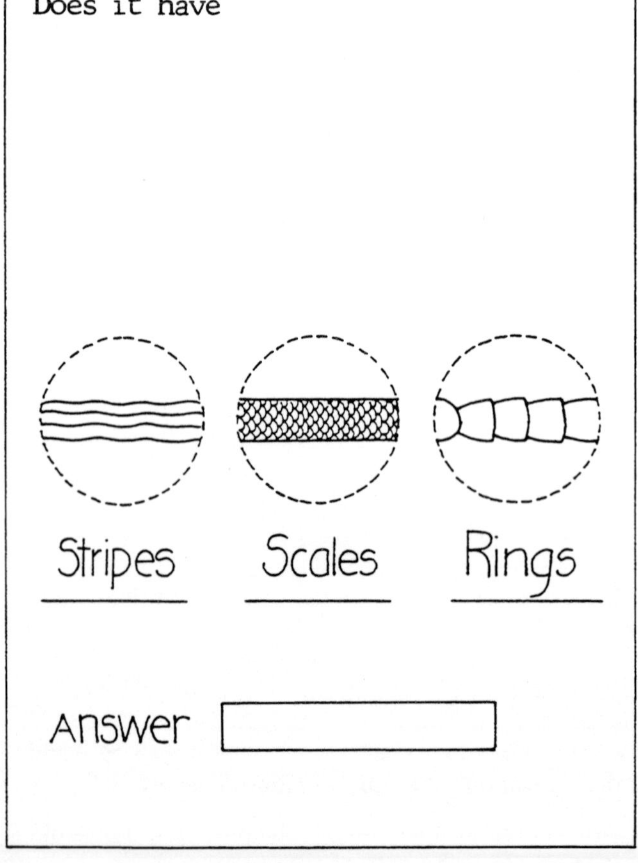

Figure 4 *Case study 2 - version A*

LOOKING AT WORMS

1. Look at a worm. Draw it here.

Measure its length ____________ mm

2. Look at the worm through the hand lens.

Does it have

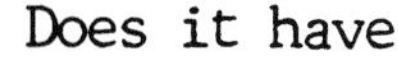

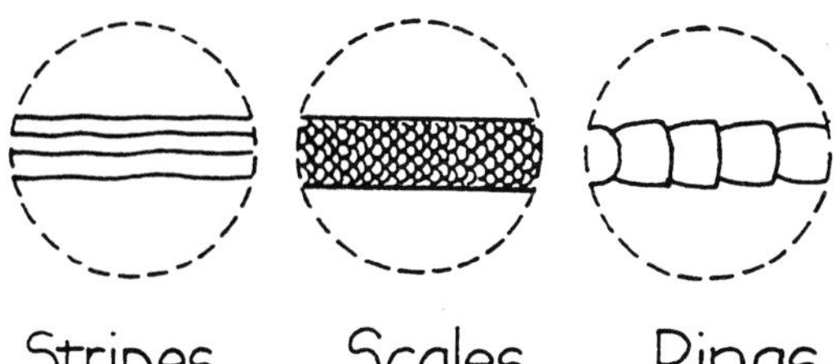

3. Stroke the belly of the worm.
Is it rough or smooth?

Look at the belly of the worm through the big lens.

Can you see the short hairs?

Draw these hairs on the diagram.

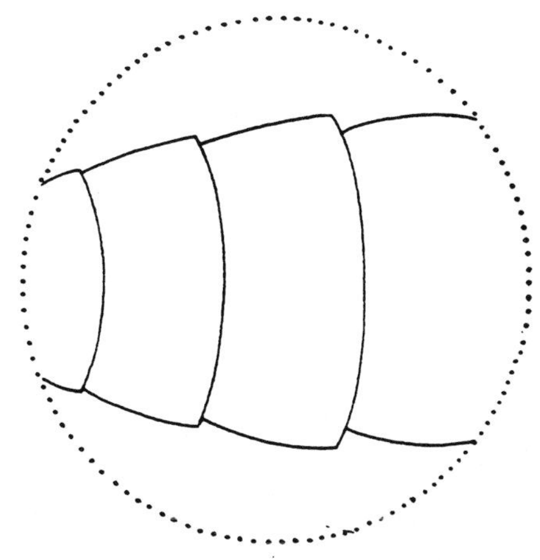

4. Watch your worm moving. Talk about this movement with your partner.
Describe the movement.

Figure 5 *Case study 2 - version B*

LOOKING AT WORMS

(a) Look at a worm. Draw it here.

Measure its length ________________ mm

(b) Look at the worm through the hand lens.

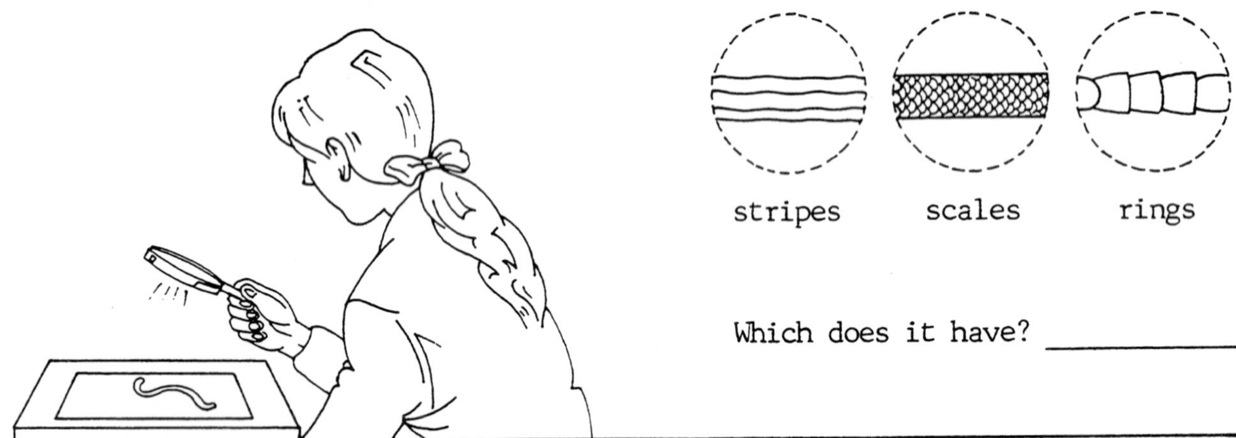

Which does it have? ____________

(c) Stroke the underside of the worm in one direction. Now stroke it in the opposite direction.
Is the underside of the worm rough or smooth?

____

Look at the underside through the big lens.
Look for the short hairs.
Draw these hairs on the diagram.

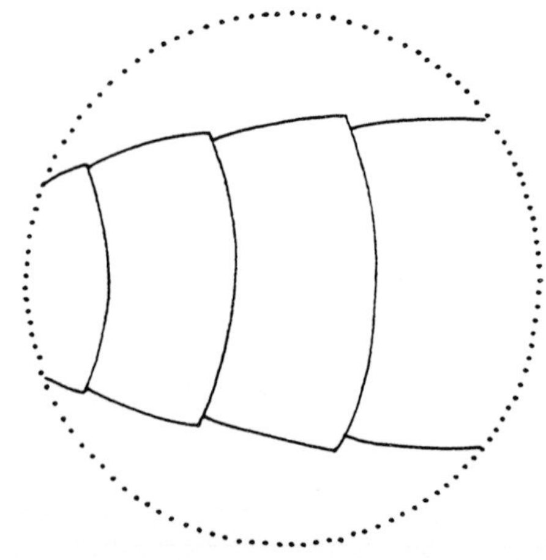

(d) Watch your worm moving. Write a description of how it moves.
These words may help you: stretch, pointed end, rounded end, flat, thin.

Figure 6 *Case study 2 - version C*

LOOKING AT WORMS

1 Look at a worm.

Draw it here.

Measure its length .... mm

2 Look at the worm through the hand lens.

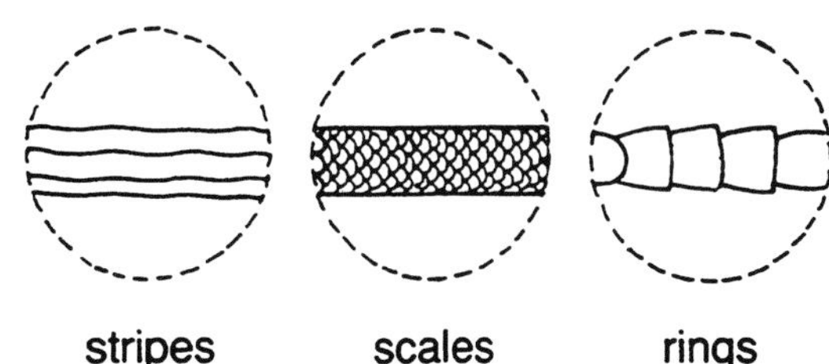

Which does it have? ....

3 Stroke the belly of the worm in one way.

Now stroke it in the other way.

Is the belly of the worm rough or smooth?

....

Look at the belly through the big lens.
Look for the short hairs.

Draw these hairs on the diagram.

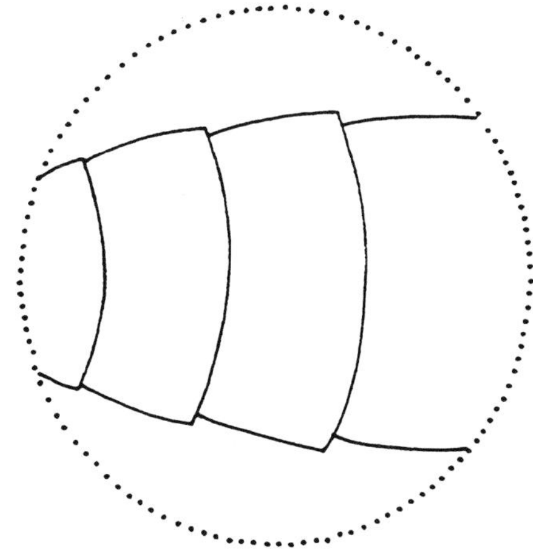

4 Watch your worm moving.

Write about how it moves. These words may help you: stretch, pointed end, rounded end, flat, thin

....

....

Figure 7 *Case study 2 – version D*

- The word 'belly' was thought to be unscientific and was changed to 'underside'.
- Field testing brought to light an obvious point: if you stroke the belly of the worm in only one direction you will not feel the bristles. Version C, therefore, directs the pupils to stroke it in both directions.

In B4 the pupils are asked to talk about the movement of the worm. The opinion of teachers was that you cannot direct pupils to talk about something – this is an activity which will occur spontaneously if the stimulus provided, the general classroom atmosphere and the physical arrangements are conducive to it. Instead, in C(d), pupils are asked to write a description and are given guidelines to help them to do this.

Later in version B (at B6, not illustrated here), reference to a 'left' and a 'right' end of the worm was thought to be meaningless. This was changed to 'rounded end' and 'pointed end'. Also, a question 'Is the worm alive?' was thought to be a stupid question. The questions in version C invite a bit more thought.

Vinegar is harmful to worms. In B7 (not illustrated) this is not emphasized. In version C the use of upper case (capitals) helps make the point.

Differences between version C and version D

The alterations in version D (Figure 7) are mainly in presentation, following the house-style of the publisher. Observe the following changes:

- the bold lettering of the title;
- the boxing of instructions to differentiate them from questions;
- the typeset text which is clearer and easier on the eye;
- the use of dotted lines for written answers, which are less confusing in their intention than straight black lines, and also less intimidating;
- the arrangement of instructions so that each starts on a new line and is clearly spaced.

In all the versions a Checkpoint has been included, where the pupil takes his worksheet to the teacher for a full check. This is a good idea. If the feedback to the pupil is inadequate, he or she may gain the idea that the responses are unimportant and lose any sense of achievement.

There is no such thing as a *perfect* worksheet. Probably you can think of a few improvements for a version E.

Chapter Three

It takes all sorts to make a world

This chapter is concerned with the problem of differentiation and the role of worksheets in a mixed-ability class. Although I concentrate here on the core and extension approach I am not implying that there is no longer a place for whole-class teaching. However, like core and extension methods, whole-class teaching is only one of a battery of strategies in the teacher's armoury to be used when appropriate.

> Where the level, pace and scope of the work were inappropriate, this was mainly because teachers failed to provide sufficient differentiation, or sometimes any differentiation at all, in the work required of pupils of different abilities . . . In a large number of cases, mixed-ability classes were taught as though they were homogenous groups. (*Mixed Ability Work in Comprehensive Schools*, HMI discussion paper, 1978)

Varying solutions have been put forward for the problem of differentiation for different ability levels:

- different *aims, skills and courses*;
- different *content*;
- different *pace*;
- different *scope and depth of study*;
- different amounts of *reinforcement*.

The notion of different levels is a complex one, because these differences vary according to different types of ability. Pupils vary in the maturity of their responses, in their confidence in oral work, in their willingness to cooperate with others; they vary in motor skills like the handling of apparatus or pronunciation of a foreign language. For most teachers, however, the problem centres on differences in cognitive ability.

This chapter discusses the core and extension approach to mixed-ability teaching in which a common core of work is completed by all pupils, followed either by remedial reinforcement for those who experience difficulties or by extension work for the more able – different scope, pace or amount of reinforcement, but same topic or area of content.

This strategy, which requires worksheets to be written at two different levels at least, should not be regarded as the sole strategy and used to the exclusion of other approaches. A balanced strategy is required which includes individualized work, group work in different types of groups, whole-class teaching, cooperative teaching and team teaching.

Remember, also, that organizing this is not something which you can do individually. There are implications for school and departmental assessment policy, for the system of reporting. And it may require timetable changes – it becomes much easier to organize and operate if you have larger blocks of time than a single 40-minute period.

There is nothing prescriptive about the model set out in Figure 8 – there are any number of variations and refinements. This model would probably be employed in about phase two of development. A phase one model might have a very simple core requiring no remedial loop and only one level of extension.

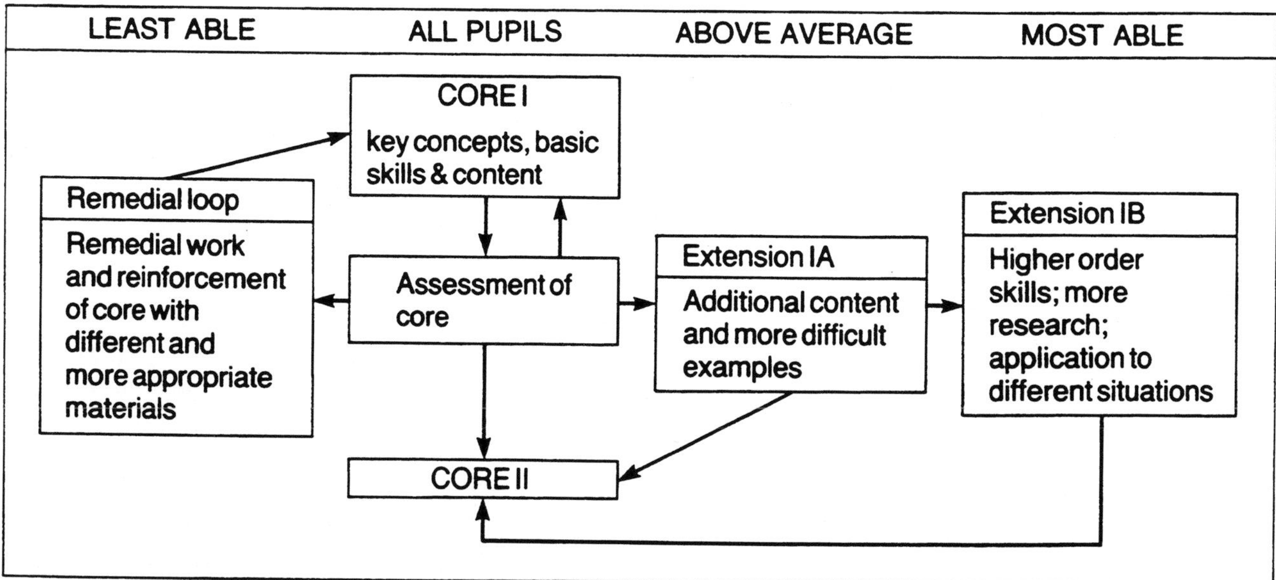

Figure 8 *One possible model of worksheet organization*

Pupils work at their own pace. In a 10-period unit, for example, some pupils may require all ten periods to complete the core and achieve the pre-set standard. Others may achieve this in about three periods and have nearly moved through Extension 1A to the end of Extension 1B.

The core

The core contains the key concepts and the basic skills and content which you regard as essential for all pupils in relation to the aims of the unit. The core should therefore be pitched at a level which all pupils can master in the time allocated to the unit. Care should be taken that the language level in instructions and worksheets, and the reading age of books used, are suitable for all pupils. The teacher preparing the core work needs to have a good idea of the pupils' previous experience of a range of skills.

At the start of the core it should be clearly stated what it is that the pupil is expected to know by the end of the core. Pupils are more likely to achieve mastery of the objectives if they know what these objectives are and exactly what they are expected to *do* to demonstrate this mastery.

Some possible alternatives

Some schools may not operate with mixed-ability classes and so some alternatives for different ranges of abilities are shown in Figure 9. The dotted lines indicate possible paths for a small minority of pupils.

Of course, the plans in Figure 9 could apply equally well to individual pupils in mixed-ability classes.

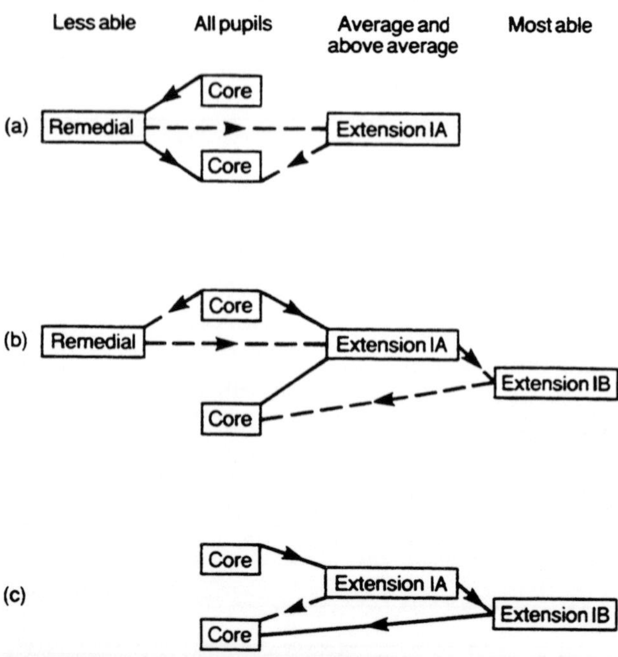

Figure 9 *Some alternative models*

On occasion you may want to supervise the class rather more closely than usual, in which case the 'concertina' approach shown in Figure 10 might be appropriate.

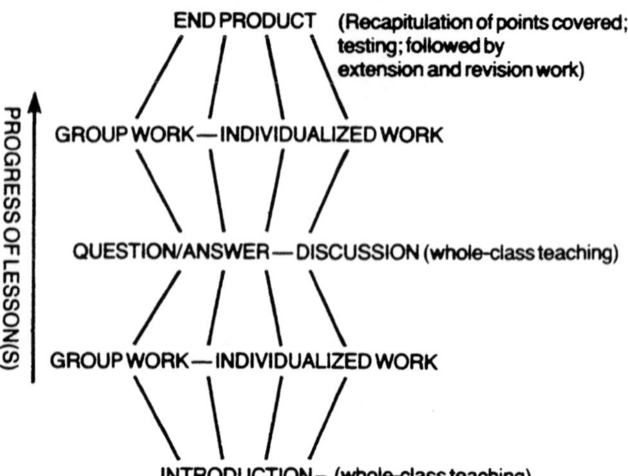

Figure 10 *The concertina approach*

The remedial loop

If the core material has been pitched at a level that is within the grasp of all the pupils in the class, why is a remedial loop necessary? Most teachers find that there are nearly always a few pupils who haven't mastered the material first time round, and that some kind of additional help is called for. This help may sometimes be more effective and efficient in a form other than that of remedial worksheets – for example, in a cooperative or team teaching situation where a second teacher is available in the classroom to give his/her full attention to the slow learners; or where there are only a small number of slow learners in the class it might be a better strategy to deal with remedial problems individually and orally rather than spend many hours devising worksheets for one or two pupils.

In constructing material for the remedial loop the learning sequence should be broken down into even smaller steps than in the core (see Example 2, p. 18); language level should be simplified; concepts should be translated from the abstract into concrete examples within the pupils' experience (see Example 3, p. 21). There should be greater use of audio-visual material, real objects and a greater variety of activity, e.g. games/simulations. Worksheets should be based on these things and not on written passages – there should be more emphasis on oral work. The construction of worksheets for less able pupils is dealt with more fully in Chapter 7.

If there is a remedial teacher in your school let him/her look at both your core material and your remedial loop. You will probably receive many useful suggestions. Ideally the remedial teacher could come into the class and work with those pupils who are on the remedial loop, if they have already been identified, while they tackle the core.

Just as the extension material should involve a degree of choice for the pupil, so should the remedial loop. This work should be just as attractive and interesting as the extension material.

Bear in mind, though, that remediation needs may well vary from pupil to pupil, so that a rigid remedial or revision scheme of work may not be the most suitable approach.

Difficulties with skills may be long-term difficulties. Once you have identified these you may wish to provide extra assistance for pupils while they are working on the core, not just when they fail to complete it.

Where difficulties relate to specific content, as well as simplifying the material try presenting it in some other way. We all learn in different ways and a different approach may bypass the 'blockage'.

When a pupil takes the core test for the second time, some teachers consider it permissible to help the less able pupil to demonstrate mastery of the core by allowing him or her to look up the answers.

A question often asked is, how many times should a pupil repeat the remedial loop? Should there be a cut-off point, or do you keep slogging away at it until mastery is obtained? The latter is called *mastery learning*. Very few teachers operate pure mastery learning; nearly all set a time limit to each unit or topic and move on before total boredom and desperation set in. The point at which one decides to move on is determined by the nature of the subject. In Mathematics or Physics, for example, it might be essential to master a formula or an equation before progressing to the next stage. But in less hierarchical subjects such as English, where one visits the same concepts, ideas or vocabulary several times over in different contexts and different units, failure to master something first time round is not quite so disastrous.

Example 1

A group of Geography teachers show how they would break certain skills into smaller steps and how extra help could be provided.

1 *Operating a questionnaire*

Verbal skills to illicit a response:	*Approach to remediation*
1 framing a question; 2 articulation of question;	Individual teacher help in framing questionnaire.
3 understanding the response:	Additional practice of questioning on each other (role playing situation).
4 accurate recording by ticking boxes.	Group activity when pupil experiences difficulties accompanied by 1 or 2 others who can 'check'.

2 *Observation/field sketching (or simulated-slide sketching)*

Skill breakdown	*Approach to remediation*
1 observation; 2 selection/ extraction of relevant data for sketch;	Additional practice in looking carefully at landscape (field or slide) and identifying the important elements, e.g. hills and valleys, rivers, buildings.
3 handling of basic tools;	Teacher shows group of pupils with difficulty in handling basic tools proper way of holding pencil, colouring etc.
4 confidence to put it down on paper.	Individual help from teacher to show how a simple sketch is built up (with OHP if in class, and using slides).

3 *Creative writing*

Skill breakdown	*Approach to remediation*
Reconstruction using language skills and technical data.	Provide pupil(s) with key words and paragraph headings. Use tape recorder, then put in note form, then written paragraph. Allow pupil(s) to rewrite paragraph from first draft. Broad approaches: allocation of more time to complete task of rewriting of first draft (with correction of spelling and grammar?).

4 *Drawing climatic graphs*

Skills breakdown	*Approach to remediation*
Pupils should be able to use the following processes:	Supply both scales in a framework, colour graphs and read off values (with examples given).
Rainfall bar graph; Temperature line graph;	
Annotating graphs with months; Creating scales for statistics.	Some columns, or temperature values, missed out; to be completed, with statistics possibly placed below each month (Figure 11).
	Blank framework, with both scales given; to be completed from table of statistics.

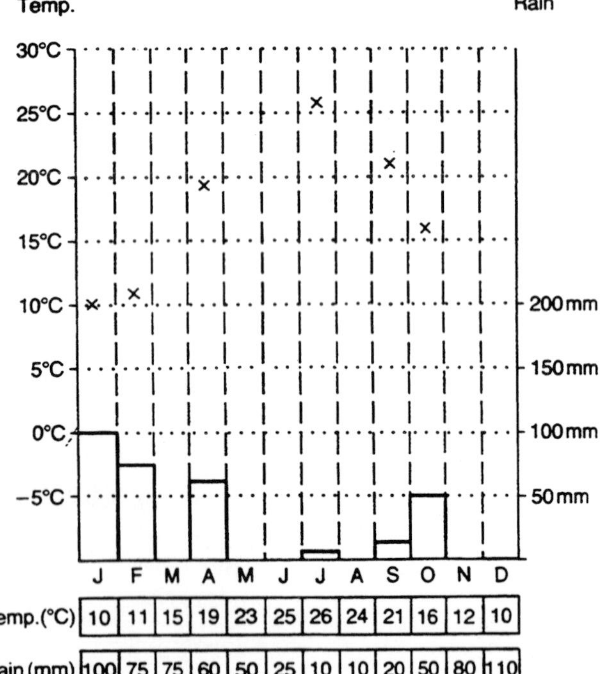

	J	F	M	A	M	J	J	A	S	O	N	D
Temp.(°C)	10	11	15	19	23	25	26	24	21	16	12	10
Rain (mm)	100	75	75	60	50	25	10	10	20	50	80	110

Figure 11 *Example 1*

Notes: (1) More gradual development possible. (2) Extension work ultimately from raw statistics, student draws framework, decides own scales, and then completes graph. (3) Graphs, where possible, should be standardized to allow comparison between home, rainforest, desert etc.

(Source: *Syllabus Construction in Geography*, conference report, Lanark Division, 1982)

Example 2

In this example, a class in their first year at secondary school were being introduced to the concept of change and were about to start studying the topic 'Changes in our society'. They began by thinking about a change that was within their immediate experience – the move from primary school to secondary school.

Figure 12 opposite shows one pupil's work.

Extension work

The purpose of extension work is to extend and challenge the more able pupils. Its purpose is not to provide more of the same, simply to fill in time until the less able have caught up. The 1978 HMI discussion paper referred to at the start of this chapter makes this point:

> Many of the examples seen failed to provide differentiation, confused pace of work with level of work by simply asking more able pupils to do more of the same in the available time, and did not offer problem-solving opportunities. Many were unchallenging, lacking academic edge, creating a superficial attitude to learning, and failing to use a wide range of references to other sources of information and ideas. . . . It seemed to HM Inspectorate that pupils of above-average ability – particularly the most able – were at the greatest disadvantage in the circumstances generally encountered in mixed-ability classes. . . . The more able were under-achieving, usually because the level of work demanded was aimed at the average or below.

There should be an opportunity to apply skills, concepts and knowledge to different situations or contexts; more individual research should be called for and more wide-ranging and challenging references used. There should be opportunities for extended writing, for evaluation and opinion, for problem-solving activities. An element of choice should be built in and different lines of investigation offered. In some cases a spiral approach can be used, revisiting the same concepts and skills as in the core, but on a higher level.

Opinions vary as to whether some objectives or skills are appropriate only to the extension, or whether all pupils should have access to all the course objectives, but on differing levels.

If your extension sheets incorporate activities in which pupils find out information for themselves, have you provided sufficient guidance on where and how to obtain this information? Have the pupils had sufficient guidance in evaluating which bits are relevant? Do not assume that pupils have reference skills, note-taking and other study skills. They may need guidance in these things. On the other hand, remember that many pupils in primary schools, through SRA reading kits etc., may be quite familiar with the core and extension approach.

	Primary Schools	Secondary School
Number of subjects		15
Number of languages study	0	0
Number of teachers	16	85
Number of rooms	16	90
school meals	went	don't go
clubs	———	———
activities after school	netball	badminton
Travel to school	bus	walk
Sport in school	football, netball etc	football, netball etc
amount of homework	little	more

Figure 12 *Example 2*

If your worksheets ask pupils to make a survey or conduct an interview, do you provide instructions on how to go about this? If your course entails pupils writing letters to firms or individuals, what steps have you taken to ensure that the receiver will not be inundated by similar letters? Is sufficient information given so that he can respond with minimum of inconvenience and expense? (E.g. pupils should not write to ask for 'everything you have on America'.)

If a report is part of a project, do you provide guidance on how it should be presented?

In time you may build up a bank of extension sheets, each with a different emphasis. From knowledge of the pupil you can then assign a particular extension to a particular pupil, or allow some choice.

You will probably find (to start with, at least) that an assessment at the end of Extension 1A and 1B (Figure 8) makes things too complicated. Nonetheless, the two extensions should be kept distinct and separate - partly because a smaller extension is less daunting for the pupil and provides a sense of achievement on completing; and partly because there should be a definite heightening in the level of work between A and B.

Often, extension work is of a problem-solving or project nature where completion of the task is, in itself, evidence of mastery.

Some general points

The core and extension approach involves more movement and more noise than is normally associated with a whole-class lesson. This, and a feeling of not being fully in control, often worries teachers who are new to this approach. However, most teachers who have tried it will agree that there are considerable benefits to be gained in providing a curriculum that suits all levels of ability and increases motivation.

With a core, two extensions and a remedial loop all in operation at the same time, there can be a great number of different worksheets in use at once. The organization and management of worksheets is discussed in Chapter 4.

A worksheet with questions of graded ability is not the same as core and extension. The difference is that the resource upon which the worksheet is based is the same for all pupils and not tailored to the needs of a particular level.

Avoid putting all the dull, slogging work in the core and all the enjoyable, 'go and find out' activities in the extension. The core should be fun too!

As time goes by and you become more used to this approach and have time to evaluate the materials you have produced, you will probably want to change a few things. For example, you may find you have included too much or too little in the core for the time allocated. As certain typical mistakes and difficulties become apparent, you will want to alter your remedial material to cater for these. You can start refining your core test so that it tells you not only which pupils are not mastering the material, but also pinpoints the nature of the difficulty. You will see possibilities for different branches and loops in the learning programme.

All hard work, but worthwhile!

I have delayed mentioning the terms until now, but what I have been discussing are *criteria-referenced* assessment and *diagnostic* assessment. These are rather daunting words and teachers often worry that they don't know enough about the techniques involved. Well, hardly anybody does! It is a developing and changing methodology. The main point is to operate your worksheets within a general strategy which gives a better deal to your pupils in a mixed-ability situation. Remember, however, that there can be pitfalls in adopting this kind of approach. In English, for example, a conventional core and extension approach with differentiated follow-up work may be less appropriate than one in which pupils have common tasks. However, different criteria are given priority depending on the stage that a pupil's general skill has reached, or more scope is given for the way that an individual interprets a task and the kind of response he can produce.

If it is the sole strategy, learning can become a very isolated experience for individual pupils, and both that and the monotonous diet of worksheets can reduce motivation. Also, use of worksheets at different levels must be handled with tact if you do not want to be continually drawing attention to the fact that some are slower learners than others.

There is the point, too, that some types of objectives can only be achieved by joint activity.

Graded tasks

The effectiveness of worksheets as part of a core and extension strategy depends a great deal on whether your judgement is right about what tasks are appropriate to core worksheets and what tasks are more suitable for extension worksheets.

In general, the factors which differentiate one level or grade of task from another are:

- For the same task/criterion/skill
    - (a) the degree of teacher support differs;
    - (b) the task is performed in a familiar/unfamiliar context;
    - (c) the task is performed at differing degrees of complexity, range or depth.
- There are additional, higher order, tasks or skills.

The following two examples demonstrate tasks which have been graded according to different levels of performance.

Example 3

The following is an extract from *Pupils with Learning Difficulties in History* by G.F. Gold, c/o Sales and Publications Unit, Jordanhill College of Education, 76 Southbrae Drive, Glasgow G13 1PP (1983):

Written activities

1 Match list of new words with list of meanings.
2 Fill in blanks from given list of words, blanks being at end of sentence.
3 Fill in blanks from given list of words, blanks in middle of sentence.
4 Fill in blanks to complete sense, blanks not confined to new or technical vocabulary, no list of possible solutions provided.
5 Give meanings of terms in pupils' own language.
6 Complete lists of factors, attributes etc., layout and some items given initially.
7 Answer a question in one sentence.
8 Answer a question using prompts or 'organizers' to develop a structure.
   e.g. How did air travel develop between 1950 and 1970?
   (Speed of aircraft, size of aircraft, numbers of passengers carried, safety, holiday travel, flying doctor services)
9 Synthesis can operate on at least two levels, namely bringing together information or ideas from two specified sources, and relating new information from a given source to material already known.
10 Write an extended answer creating own structure.

Example 4

Table 3 is an extract from the guidelines for the Science course for the new Scottish Certificate of Education. The new certificate is based on a 7-point scale (7 being the bottom of the scale).

The example shows the grade-related criteria, worked out for information-handling skills and used for differentiating between points 2, 5 and 6 on the scale.

Table 3

HANDLING INFORMATION - EXTENDED GRC

Grade 6	*Grade 5*	*Grade 2*
A pupil awarded this Grade will have demonstrated ability to:	*In addition*, a pupil obtaining this Grade will have demonstrated ability to:	*In addition*, a pupil obtaining this Grade will have demonstrated ability to:
6.1 locate information by using the index of a book;		2.1 distinguish the main theme of a piece of scientific writing;
6.2 obtain relevant information from a given simple source, to include a passage of writing, picture, key and flow chart;	5.2 obtain and collate information from a number of suggested sources, to include a passage of writing, picture, key and flow chart;	2.2 extract and collate information from a variety of self-sought sources;
6.3 extract relevant data from one given source at a time, to include a table, diagram, key, flow chart, bar graph, pie chart and line graph;	5.3 extract relevant data from pre-selected sources, to include a table, diagram, key, flow chart, bar graph, pie chart and line graph;	2.3 extract relevant data from a number of sources, to include tables, diagrams, keys, flow charts, bar graphs, pie charts and line graphs;
6.4 present information in written form, identifying a purpose or idea;	5.4 present information in written form, identifying the main purpose or idea;	2.4 present information in written form and identify the main purpose or idea clearly and concisely;
6.5 complete tables of data when the headings are given;	5.5 construct tables of data selecting appropriate headings;	
6.6 draw and label diagrams;	5.6 draw and label simple pie charts;	
6.7 complete flow charts, keys, bar graphs and line graphs;	5.7 construct bar graphs and line graphs given the scales and the axes;	2.7 construct pie charts and line graphs when scales and axes are not given;
6.8 solve science-based problems involving one operation from addition, subtraction, multiplication and division applied in a familiar situation;	5.8 carry out metric conversions of scientific units;	2.8 solve problems involving at least two operations;
6.9 use given percentages in science-based situations.		2.9 express one quantity as a percentage of another.
	5.10 calculate the average value of a series of measurements	

Point 5 is the overlap point between a 'Foundation Level' course and a 'General Level' course (equivalent to 'O' level).

Point 2 is the overlap point between 'General Level' and 'Credit Level' (approximately the top 20 per cent of the 15–16 age group).

The guidelines recommend that, within the part of the syllabus designed for the less able pupils (the Foundation Course) modules be operated on a core and extension basis. Grade 5 is suggested as appropriate for core work and Grade 6 for extension work.

Case study 3
Figure 13 is from a Mathematics 'Foundation' course for 15-year-olds. It shows how a higher level of objective could be achieved by asking the same question, but in a different order. In version A the pupil is only required to proceed through the clues from the beginning to the end. In version B the pupil has first to create a sequence of steps and work out a very simple network diagram before proceeding.

Case study 4
The remainder of this chapter shows an extract from a unit about the imaginary Utherton By-pass, the unit being part of a course entitled *Co-operation and Conflict* (Dunbarton Modern Studies Working Party for First and Second years, 1982).

This extract looks at the concept of Protest. It was aimed at pupils of ages 12–13.

The material is presented at three levels, the core (the first four sheets), the revision (remedial) exercises, and the extension exercises. They are labelled here Figures 14, 15 and 16 respectively.

Please study these sheets (pp. 23–31) before reading my comment which follows.

Comment on the 'Protest' worksheets
In the original material the core sheets were yellow, the revision sheets green and the extension sheet pink.

The core. Note the following points:

1 The aims of the lesson are explained to the pupil.
2 The worksheet addresses the pupil personally: 'I', 'me', 'you'.
3 There are none of the usual blank-filling exercises.
4 Exercise 17 requires the pupil to process the information by digesting it in pictorial form and delivering it in sentence form.
5 In Exercise 19 the badge is much too small for making a design on.
6 The word banks are placed on the pages where the words are used, rather than at the end.

Version A

Complete this number puzzle

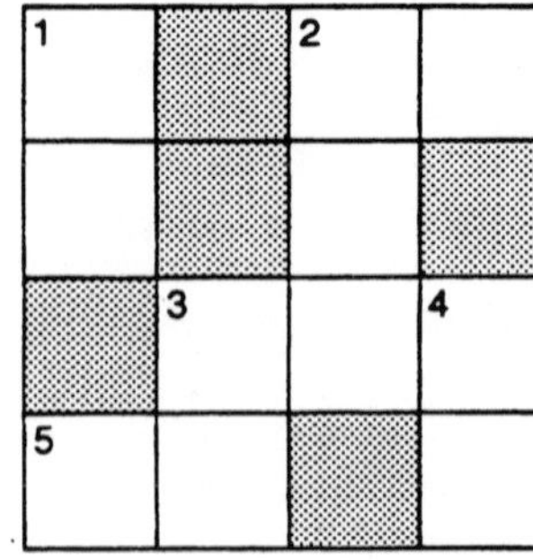

CLUES ACROSS
(2) 500 minus 453
(3) 70 plus 66
(5) 7 × 10

CLUES DOWN
(1) Half of 136
(2) 187 + 266
(3) The number of mm in one centimetre
(4) 4 less than 70

Version B

CLUES ACROSS
(2) 500 minus 2-down
(3) 5-across plus 4-down
(5) 7 × 10

CLUES DOWN
(1) Half of 3-across
(2) 187 + 266
(3) The number of mm in one centimetre
(4) 4 less than 5-across

Figure 13 *Case study 3*

The revision sheets.
1 'Revision' is more friendly than 'remedial'.
2 The revision sheets concentrate on Exercises 16 and 20 because these are the exercises upon which this part of the core test is based.

The extension sheets. These sheets attempt to look at the actual mechanics of protest in more detail, to use real source materials, and to guide pupils towards extracting relevant information from a piece of adult prose. Some teachers who have used this unit comment that there aren't enough extension sheets and that their most able pupils run out of things to do.

Table 4 compares the words used to direct pupil tasks and exercises in the core and in the extension.

Table 4

Core	Extension	
Tick the box (implied)	Imagine	Explain
Complete the sentence (implied)	Write	List
Match up	Express	Suggest
Design	Point out	Find out
Which?	Look at	Notice

PRESSURE GROUPS

PROTEST

This section will help you to know:-

- Why you would have a right to protest about something like the by-pass.
- What a pressure group is.
- Why joining a pressure group might be a good way of protesting.

YOU HAVE A RIGHT TO PROTEST

- You are paying for the by-pass through rates and taxes.
- You voted for the Regional Council who are making the decisions about the by-pass.

By law, details about any plans for a by-pass must be made known to the public, so that they can protest if they want to.

Exercise 16

True or False?

I have no right to protest about a by-pass because the government is paying for it. | True | False |

The Regional Council don't need to tell anyone if they are planning a by-pass. | True | False |

The Regional Council was elected by the people in the Region. What the Regional Council decide to do is therefore my business. | True | False |

What the Regional Council decide is nothing to do with me. | True | False |

By law, the Regional Council must tell the public if they are planning a by-pass. | True | False |

I have a right to protest if I want to. | True | False |

Figure 14(a) *Case study 4 - core sheet*

PRESSURE GROUPS

The planners and decision-makers are more likely to take notice of well organized, united groups than of individuals. Such groups are called "pressure groups".

INDIVIDUAL ACTION

A PRESSURE GROUP

EXERCISE 17

People join pressure groups because

____

____

____

____

WORD BANK

INDIVIDUAL: Single, separate, on your own.

Figure 14(b) *Case study 4 – core sheet*

WORD BANK	
ABOLITION:	putting an end to something; doing away with something.
PLACARD:	a poster carried on a board.

Exercise 18

Match up these two columns.

PRESSURE GROUP		WHAT THEY ARE TRYING TO DO
National Union of Mineworkers	☐	A. Do away with the belt
Friends of the Earth	☐	B. Better conditions for motorists
Automobile Association (AA)	☐	C. Protection of the environment
Anti-Blood Sports Society	☐	D. No foxhunting
Scottish Teachers opposed to Physical Punishment (STOP)	☐	E. Better conditions for miners
Campaign for Nuclear Disarmament	☐	F. Ban all nuclear weapons

Exercise 19

Design a placard and a badge for one of the groups mentioned above.

Figure 14(c) *Case study 4*

Exercise 20

Four of the following are pressure groups. Which are they?

Ban the By-Pass Action Group.. ☐

Utherton Ladies Knitting Circle.................................... ☐

Wildlife Preservation Society...................................... ☐

SSPCA (Scottish Society for Prevention of Cruelty to Animals)... ☐

The Plastic Mac Pop Group.. ☐

Campaign for Nuclear Disarmament................................. ☐

Tufty Club.. ☐

Utherton Amateur Dramatic Society................................ ☐

Figure 14(d) *Case study 4*

REVISION

Exercise 7

Turn to Core Exercise 16 of page 15 of the core booklet.

Cut out the box below. Then cut out the black squares.

Place the box exactly over the True/False answers on figure 14(a). This will tell you which are the correct answers.

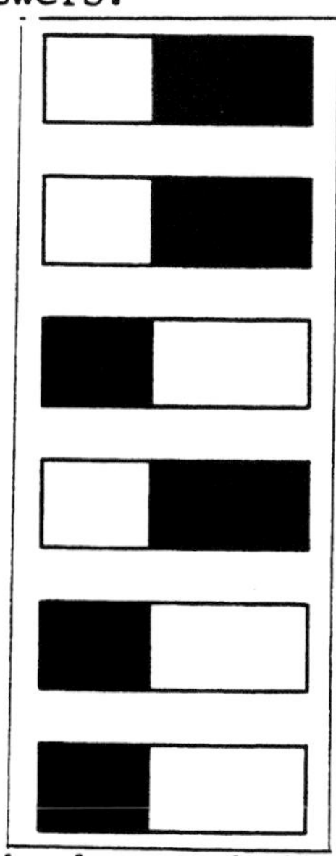

Now try Core Exercise 16 without the box to help you.

Exercise 8

Study the sentences below before trying Core Exercise 20.

1. Joining a pressure group can be a good way of protesting about something and trying to change what is happening.
2. The Ban-the-By-Pass Action Group is a pressure group. What are they protesting about? ....
3. The Wildlife Preservation Society is a pressure group. What are people in the group trying to do? ....
4. The SSPCA is a pressure group. What do the letters SSPCA stand for? (page 18 of the core booklet will tell you)........................
   ....
5. The Campaign for Nuclear Disarmament is a pressure group. What are they protesting about? ....
   What are they trying to do about it?..............................
   ....
   ....

Now try doing Core Exercise 20 on page 18 of the core booklet

Figure 15 *Case study 4 – revision sheet*

UTHERTON BY-PASS

Extension Exercise

1. Imagine that you are a concerned member of a pressure group which is against the Utherton by-pass. Write a letter to the editor of "The Utherton News", expressing the point of view of your group.
2. Imagine that you are a citizen of Utherton who is in favour of the by-pass. Write a letter to the Utherton News pointing out the advantages of the by-pass.
3. Look at the form headed 'Development Application Report'. (Document A).
   - (i) What are the Acts of Parliament which state that this consultation procedure must be followed?
   - (ii) Explain in your own words the meaning of 'consultation'.
   - (iii) List five official departments or organizations mentioned in Document A which must be consulted.
   - (iv) The blank spaces under 'consultations' are for local groups and organizations which wish to be consulted. Suggest two groups in Utherton which might be consulted.
   - (v) Who has to sign this form?
4. Here is a real example of the reply made by a local organization when consulted about the Bonhill by-pass (near Alexandria). See Document B.
   - (i) What is the name of the group which is making observations (comments or suggestions) about the Bonhill by-pass?
   - (ii) Write down the suggestions which concern the safety of the community.
   - (iii) Find out the meaning of the word 'amenity'.
   - (iv) Write down the suggestions which concern amenities for the local community.
5. The Regional Council is required by law to inform the public of plans for new developments and to give the public a chance to make comments, raise objections etc. Document C is the public notice which was put in local newspapers informing the public about the Bonhill by-pass.
   - (i) If you wanted to see the plans for the by-pass, where would you go?
   - (ii) If you wanted to make a representation, to whom should you write? What is the time limit allowed for receiving such letters?

Figure 16(a) *Case study 4 - extension sheet*

Document A	Form 10 DEPARTMENT OF PLANNING & DEVELOPMENT Town & Country Planning (Scotland) Acts, 1947/74	
Code		No. ....
Cert.		Date ....
I.D.C.	DEVELOPMENT APPLICATION REPORT by Director of Planning & Development	O/S No. ....
Date of Meeting		Grid Ref. ....

APPLICANT			AGENT		
SITE Area			PROPOSAL Density		
Acknowledged			Recorded on B.S.3.		

GENERAL INFORMATION

D.P.Zoning	Existing Use
Programming	Condition
Action Area	Listed Building
Road Proposals	Site Inspection/Initialled
Previous Applications	General Remarks

CONSULTATIONS	Date OUT	Date IN	Comment
Director of Physical Planning, Strathclyde Region			
☐ Drainage Authority			
☐ Roads Authority			
☐ Building Control Section			
☐ Dept. of Environmental Health			
☐ Adjoining Planning Authority			
☐ Water Authority			
☐ Director of Architectural Services			
☐ Countryside Commission			
☐ The Senior Lands Officer — D.A.F.S.			
☐ River Purification Board			
☐			
☐			
☐			

Figure 16(b) *Case study 4 – extension sheet*

Document A (cont'd)

STRUCTURAL DETAILS (Form 10)

DOCUMENTS TO COMMITTEE

..........sets of ....plans ....Consultation Reports Certificate...........

.... Application Forms ....Forms B .....Wayleave Forms

---

RECOMMENDATION TO COMMITTEE

SUGGESTED CONDITIONS/REASONS (for refusal, limitation, conditions etc.)

FURTHER ACTION REQUIRED

MINUTED [ ] ....

Figure 16(c) *Case study 4 – extension sheet*

Document B

DUMBARTON DISTRICT COUNCIL

Our Ref. VL. 2993 Date 30.1.81.

Name of Applicant: Strathclyde Regional council, per D.McIntyre, Strathclyde Regional Council, Regional Offices, Cotton Street, Paisley

Nature of Proposal: Road Improvement/re-alignment.

Site: A313 Bonhill.

TOWN AND COUNTRY PLANNING (SCOTLAND) ACTS, 1947/74

OBSERVATIONS OF Bonhill Community Council,

1. Provision of a crossing at Burn Street.
2. Footpaths along length.
3. Traffic barriers both sides Ladyton.
4. Control of speed on road at Ladyton.
5. Will existing bus service still go through old Bonhill?
6. Will premises being demolished, in particular shops, be replaced?

Document C

COUNTY REPORTER, WEDNESDAY, 21st JANUARY. 1981

PUBLIC NOTICES

TOWN AND COUNTRY PLANNING (SCOTLAND) ACT 1972

NOTICE UNDER SECTION 23 (2)

PROPOSED DEVELOPMENT AT BONHILL

Notice is hereby given that application is being made to the Dumbarton District Council by the Strathclyde Regional Council for planning permission in respect of road improvement at Route A313 Bonhill.

A copy of the application and of the plans and other documents submitted with it may be inspected at all reasonable hours at the Planning Department Council Offices, Garshake Road, Dumbarton, during the period of 21 days beginning with the date of publication of this notice.

Any person who wishes to make representations to the above mentioned Council about the application should make them in writing within that period to the Council at Director of Administration, Dumbarton District Council, Crasslet House, Argyll Avenue, Dumbarton.

(Sgd.) ROBERT CALDERWOOD
on behalf of
The Strathclyde Regional Council
16th January, 1981.

Figure 16(d) *Case study 4 – extension sheet*

Chapter Four

Blame the management

It's all too easy for one's worksheets to get into a muddle. They can't be found, they get into the wrong order and into the wrong piles, they run out just when you need them. This chapter is about the organization and management of worksheets at departmental and classroom levels. I would hope that some of the points I make are helpful in themselves, but since this book is supposed to be about the writing and production of worksheets, let me say that you need to be clear about what the organization and management arrangements are *before* you start production because these arrangements will influence such things as the headings you adopt, the identification/classification marks at the top of the worksheet, what kind of directions you include on the worksheet for the pupil, and the colour of paper you use.

Departmental policy

Every subject department should have a clearly understood policy within which worksheets are operated. Any such policy should cover the following points:

- Compatability with any more centralized systems, e.g. a School Resource Centre, School Library, Faculty Resource Centre.
- The role of ancillary staff (if any), e.g. technicians, auxiliaries, librarians, laboratory staff. The role of such persons may go well beyond setting up, fetching, carrying and putting away things. Librarians, for example, have a very positive role in teaching pupils enquiry and reference skills. Similarly, laboratory staff might well be involved in assisting pupils to organize materials for experiments or helping them to use special equipment. Obviously there is greater educational value in such situations if the staff concerned have been given an understanding of the basic aims and methods of the course.
- A system of storage and retrieval for resources held within the departmental base and a system for managing worksheets within the classroom. These aspects are dealt with more fully in the next section, but the point needs to be made here that teaching methods such as resource-based learning, individual enquiry and group work will not operate effectively on a system of storage and retrieval which is organized for whole-class teaching.

I am convinced that in the subjects which rely on printed sources one of the most potent decisions that a Head of Department makes is how to organize his stocks of teaching material, for the method of teaching is strongly influenced by this. And I am further convinced that it is in the direction of variety, flexibility, and availability, with the concomitant requirements of full cataloguing, careful stock checking and efficient issuing, that each Head of Department must be moving! (*Head of Department* by Michael Marland, Heinemann Educational Books, 1971)

- A clear understanding about who is responsible for the worksheets in each year group. Such responsibility should cover: replenishing supplies, making sure that the system is being operated as it should be, regular checks to ensure that everything is in its proper place.
- Procedures for evaluation of worksheets, review and update of content and of allied resources.
- Procedures for review and update of the general resource management policy – which might need to change as the curriculum changes, as the departmental budget changes, as new technology opens up new possibilities.
- Clear arrangements for the hiring/booking of films and other audio-visual aids from organizations outside the school. This avoids situations such as the same film being ordered three times over by different members of the department – or nobody ordering it.
- A policy about what materials can be taken home by teachers (for preparation, familiarization etc.) and what cannot.
- A regular review of timetabling requirements. Resource-based learning and core and extension methods are very difficult to operate within a single 40-minute period. Even in a smooth-running classroom with well-trained pupils, the time spent in organizing and laying out the resources at the start of the class and of tidying up at the end, demands a bigger block of time than the traditional single period provides.
- An agreed schedule for who is teaching which unit when. This way, the number of worksheets required at one time can be forecast. If possible, some kind of rota system should be used with only, say, a third of the year group doing the same unit at any one time. Not only does this avoid undue strain being put on available resources, it also allows pitfalls to be discovered, mistakes ironed out etc., and avoided by the remaining two-thirds.

Departmental organization

Most of the cataloguing, indexing and retrieval systems described in the literature on resources are designed for school or area resource centres and are too complex and too time-consuming to set up for the limited resources of a single department.

Some of the best run departments that I know store their worksheets in old shoe boxes or boxes that once held A4 paper. The point is that these boxes are clearly labelled and are part of a system that relates to all the other resources relevant to the course, that is easy to operate and is understood by all in the department.

Any system of managing resources would be helped by having:

- a visual plan/chart showing where all the resources are located;
- a central departmental catalogue of resources held in stock;
- a scheme of work which details the related resource material available;
- for each teacher involved and for each course, a complete set of worksheets in a loose-leaf binder.

Labelling worksheets

The contents of the boxes, drawers or files that contain the worksheets are probably best identified by using the same label as on the worksheet.

The identifying label from the top of a worksheet might be as follows:

S3/CS/3/E2.2/B4
(i) (ii) (iii) (iv) (v)

(i) indicates the year group, i.e. 3rd year of secondary school; (ii) the title of the course/unit (Changing Society); (iii) the number of the sub-unit/section; (iv) extension exercise 2, page 2 (if, for example, it had been core exercise 3, page 1, the label would have been C3.1); (v) the type of sheet it is – in this case it is source element number 4, B simply being a code letter according to the following list:

A = worksheet
B = source extract
C = fact sheet
D = text
E = visual sheet (photograph, picture, cartoon etc.)
F = teacher information sheet

The same information could be arranged in a different way, as in Figure 17(a). Going one step further, a written identification (Figure 17(b)) has the advantage of being more immediately intelligible and more easily understood by the main user, i.e. the pupil. Lastly, in the example in Figure 17(c) a symbol has been used to identify the type of

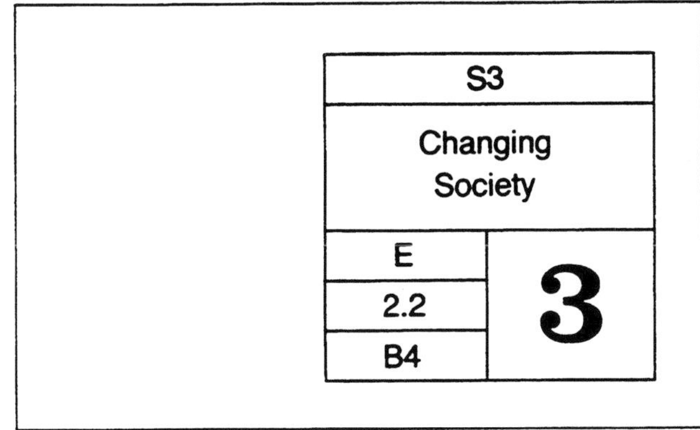

Figure 17(a) *Worksheet labelling*

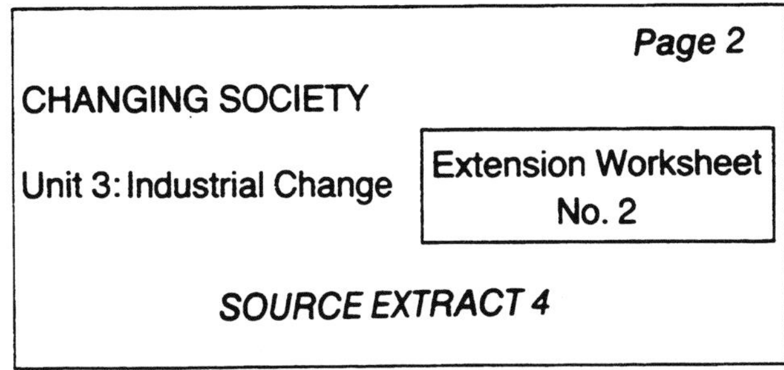

Figure 17(b) *Worksheet labelling*

THE AMERICAN WEST
Unit 4
The Miners

Figure 17(c) *Worksheet labelling*

sheet it is. The fact that it is on white paper indicates that it is a core worksheet. In this particular case, the colour coding was as follows:

white = core
yellow = remedial
green = extension
grey = teacher information

Keeping track of worksheets and maintaining them in their correct order becomes much easier if each unit or sub-unit is bound together in one booklet. If the cover is labelled, the separate sheets need less information at the top of each. However, there are disadvantages to the booklet format:

- If you are building in to your course alternative routes and choice and flexibility in the use of the worksheets, you may have to include a lot of material in each booklet which will not be used by every pupil.
- Many courses undergo constant evaluation, revision and change. If worksheets are being replaced from year to year, the work involved in collating and stapling your booklets may not be worthwhile.

The departmental catalogue

There are a number of ways of arranging a catalogue, e.g. by the Dewey Decimal System, alphabetically by topic, by author or by the type of media. Personally I favour a system that gives fairly broad topic or theme headings, which lists the same resource in several different parts of the catalogue if it is relevant to different headings, and which treats all resources, including worksheets, in this way.

If your department has access to a microcomputer, the time spent putting your resource information on to disc is well worth while. The speed of information retrieval, the vastly increased potential for cross-referencing and the ease of update make this an extremely useful tool.

Example 5
This example, from the English Department at Heywood Senior High School, gives a good idea of the kind of information that a catalogue might contain (see Figure 18 opposite), although it was devised for the information of a school resource centre rather than a departmental catalogue.

Storage of worksheets

Apart from in properly labelled boxes or cabinet drawers, a good way of storing worksheets is in a suspended system such as Railex. This allows the storage of duplicating stencils as well. If worksheets are suspended in plastic wallets or bags, they are easily identified and the actual number of worksheets in stock can be seen at a glance.

The organization of worksheets in the classroom

A key decision is whether you use your worksheets and their accompanying resources on an open access or a closed access system. Open access means that the material may be found by the pupil without it having to be fetched for, or handed out to, him or her.

For anything but whole-class teaching open access is advisable. Not only will you save yourself from non-stop pestering for this item or that; but also, locating information, following written instructions and setting up equipment are all valid educational aims. The more pupils feel that they are being given a measure of independence and have a responsibility for their own learning, the better their motivation.

Some items might be held on closed access for various reasons: you might want to give special advice to the pupil before he uses it; you might want to use a particular item as a check-point so that, when a pupil asks for it, you know he has progressed to that particular stage; or it might be susceptible to damage.

This 'self-service' element operates successfully in many classrooms. Fairly typically the worksheets are contained in folders which are either pinned around the walls or kept in open cupboards and the pupils select the appropriate worksheets/materials as needed. Another approach is the 'stations' approach. The worksheets and equipment appropriate to particular tasks or experiments are set out in different parts of the classroom or laboratory. Or again, for group work, each group is provided with a folder.

Systems like this operate most effectively when there has been positive training for pupils in how to play their part. Pupils should know:

- how the system works – the meanings of words like 'core' and 'extension';
- precisely what they have to do when certain written instructions appear on their worksheets;
- when to seek help from the teacher and when to seek help from each other;
- where materials and equipment are located;
- how to operate simple items of equipment;
- what to do when equipment is missing or faulty, or containers empty;
- what the assessment procedures are and how to operate self-marking procedures;
- how to chart their own progress.

ENGLISH FEATURE LIST

Originator .... Description of Material Accession Number ....

Is stencil held? YES/NO

Date material deposited ....

WHAT SORT OF THING IS IT?

Book
Book extract
Building
Chart
Cineloop
Single copy
Multiple copy
Diagram
Exam paper

Film
Filmstrip
Gramophone record
Illustration/Drawing
Magazine article
Magazine extract
Map
Model
Newspaper cutting

Society/Organization
Pamphlet
Person
Photograph
Place
Questionnaire
Sheet music
Slide(s)
Specimen(s)
Study Guide (multiple copies)

Study Guide (single copy)
Study pack/Kit
Syllabus
Tape
Tape cassette
Teacher's notes
OHP transparency
Videotape
Worksheet
Pupil produced

WHERE IS THE ITEM STORED?

Filmstrip cabinet
Tape library cabinet
Slide cabinet
Chart/Poster cabinet
Display/Picture cabinet

Study kit shelves
Reference shelves
Periodical shelves
English Department

TREATMENT

Autobiography
Abstract
Argument
Bibliography
Biography
Criticism
Documentary

Outline
Narrative
Statistics
Translation
Verse
Vocal
Audio/Lingual

TREATMENT - ORIGINATOR'S JUDGEMENT

Difficult to understand - (ideas)
Difficult to understand - (vocabulary)
Easy to understand

Biassed
Moving
Factually suspect

FOR USE WITH WHICH AGE GROUP?

Middle school - 3rd/4th Years
5th year CSE
5th Year GCE

6th Form 'A' and 'S'
6th Form General

PERIOD COVERED BY MATERIAL

Before 500 A.D.
500 A.D. - 1500 A.D.
1500 - 1600
1601 - 1700

1701 - 1800
1801 - 1900
1900 - 1950
1950 onwards

TOPICS (not listed here)

Figure 18 *Example 5*

Keeping track of things

With three levels of worksheets being used at once and pupils working at different paces, keeping track of where everyone has got to in the unit can present problems.

Figure 19 is an example of a simple system for recording which worksheets each pupil has done. Pupils can be trained to keep a similar personal record and to enter their progress on a master chart on the classroom wall.

Another method is to keep a class list beside each pile or wallet of worksheets on which pupils can tick their names each time they take a new worksheet.

Build regular checkpoints into your worksheets, with instructions which say 'when you reach this point come to me to have your work checked'. And put a box for your signature and the date.

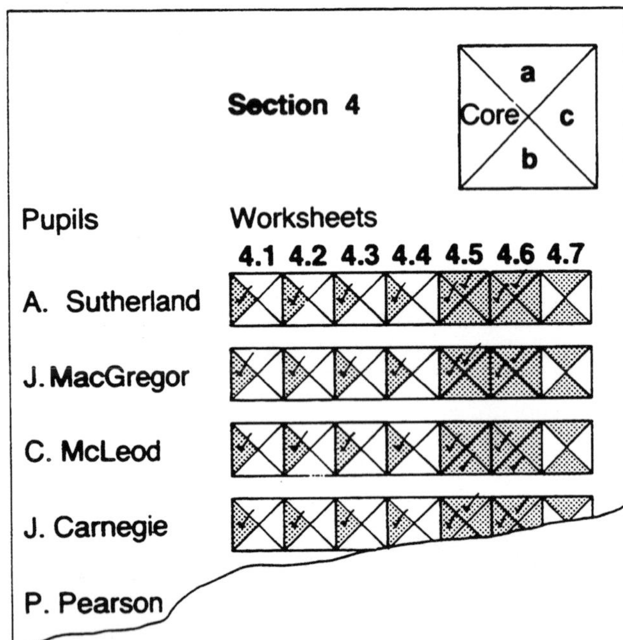

Figure 19 *Simple system for recording completed worksheets*

Case study 5

This case study is drawn from the SRA Junior Reading for Understanding Programme. It shows how pupils can take responsibility for checking their own work, recording their results and charting their own progress.

Figure 20 shows the first side of a ten-question lesson card. The number 15 indicates the step. There are 100 steps in the programme. Each step has four lesson cards, marked by a symbol: a circle, a diamond, a square or a triangle.

Figure 21 is an extract from the answer key booklet, used by each pupil to check responses to the lesson card. Thus, for step 15 of the diamond card, the correct response to question 1 is B ('burn'), and to question 2 it is D ('day').

◇ 15

1 Through the magnifying glass, the rays of the sun came together on one little spot on the paper. The paper got so hot that it began to

A – tear. **B** – burn. **C** – melt. **D** – crack.

2 February is the shortest month of the year; every four years it has an extra

A – week. **B** – holiday. **C** – Friday. **D** – day.

3 Many drivers do not like to take long trips alone because it is hard for them to stay awake. If they have a companion on the trip, they like this person to talk to them. If they drive alone, they are more like to

A – go to sleep. **C** – drive at night.
B – turn off the radio. **D** – stay on the road.

4 Americans are very much interested in westerns – movies, TV programs, stories, history, songs, and games. It is not only children who show this interest. Adults may not play cowboys and Indians themselves, but they like to watch the TV western shows. Westerns are popular with

A – persons of all ages. **C** – Indians.
B – young women. **D** – Europeans.

5 The postman always comes regardless of the weather. We can always

A – pay him. **C** – depend on him.
B – write to him. **D** – hear him.

Figure 20 *Case study 5*

	11	12	13	14	15
No.	●◆■▲	●◆■▲	●◆■▲	●◆■▲	●◆■▲
1	A B B B	D B A B	D A B D	C D B D	D B B D
2	B C C C	D D A B	C B A A	D C D C	C D A B
3	D D D B	B B B A	D C C A	A B A A	B A D A
4	C D D C	C C A D	A C C B	C A D A	A A A A
5	B A B A	B A B A	B D C C	D A C A	B C D B
6	C B C A	D D B B	A B D A	B D A B	C D B C
7	C B C A	D B D D	A C A D	C A D D	C D C D
8	A C A D	D B D D	C A B C	A D D D	D A A C
9	A A B D	B C C D	B B A A	D C C D	C C C C
10	B C A C	A C B A	C D D C	D B B A	B B C A

Figure 21 *Extract from answer key booklet*

The pupil then records his or her results, according to instructions, as in Figure 22. The instructions printed on the record card are as follows:

- When you have finished take an answer key booklet from the box. Compare your answers with the answers in the key booklet. Place a tick mark (✓) on

RECORD OF READING PRACTICES

Practice 1		Practice 2	
DATE March 1		DATE March 3	
○ ◇(15) □ △		○ ◇ □(15) △	
1	B	1 B	✓
2	✓	2 A	✓
3	A	3 (C)	D
4	✓	4 A	✓
5	C	5 (A)	D
6	✓	6 B	✓
7	✓	7 C	✓
8	✓	8 A	✓
9	C	9 C	✓
10	✓	10 (A)	C
TOTAL RIGHT 6		TOTAL RIGHT 7	

Figure 22 *Pupil's own marking chart*

the line after each correct answer. Encircle each incorrect answer.

- Count the number of correct answers. Write this number at the bottom of the practice chart.
- If your answer is incorrect, write the correct answer beside it. Then read the paragraph again and try to see why your answer was incorrect. You will usually be able to see why your answer is wrong. If you do not you should ask your teacher to explain. If you understand why you were wrong, you will make fewer mistakes next time.

The pupil subsequently records progress on a progress chart (Figure 23). The text in the pupils' instruction booklet says:

To see how you are progressing, look at the bars on the graph. If your bars make an even line down the page you are improving. Tell your teacher when you have worked

(a) two days on one step with scores of 9 or 10, or
(b) two days on one step with scores below 6.

The pupil is improving if he or she scores much the same each time (if the bars make an even line down the page), because the exercises become progressively more difficult.

Avoiding bottlenecks

The problem usually occurs when a large proportion of the class (usually the average-ability or middle-of-the-class pupils) all finish a section at much the same time and want their work checked or a test marked.

The more training you give pupils in 'self-servicing' the less of a problem this becomes. Remember that the kind of system we looked at in the SRA case study is often operated successfully by primary school children.

In certain instances, it can be of mutual educational benefit for the fast learners in the class to help the slow learners in checking their work.

SAMPLE PROGRESS CHART

LESSON				NUMBER RIGHT									
●	◆	■	▲	1	2	3	4	5	6	7	8	9	10
	15												
		15											
15													
			15										
16													
	16												
		16											
			16										
	17												
		17											
			17										
18													
	18												
		19											
19													
	20												
			20										
		20											
20													
		21											

Figure 23 *Sample progress chart*

Use your professional judgement to decide when.

Marking tests can be speeded up by the layout of the page, e.g. if the responses are always in the same position on the page. For one-word answers or for boxes marked with a tick etc., a marking grid or overlay can be devised. An example of this is given in Chapter 5.

Chapter Five

By their worksheets you shall know them

Assessment is a vast subject with many facets. This chapter is about one small aspect of that subject - the role of worksheets in assessment. Emphasis will be put upon formative assessment generally and criterion referenced assessment in particular, because the educational current is running strongly in these directions. Early in 1984 the Government outlined proposals for an examination system that would measure pupils against set levels of achievement. In Scotland this trend is already under way with the implementation of the Munn and Dunning reports and the phased introduction of the new 14–16 Standard Grade Examination based upon Grade Related Criteria. Previous chapters have discussed core and extension methods. These, too, assume a commitment to formative assessment and criterion referencing.

What, exactly, do these terms mean?

Formative assessment is very much part of the learning situation and the information gained from the assessment is used for diagnostic purposes and as feedback to the learner. Summative assessment is concerned with a final summing up, with making judgements about the pupil for use by people other than the learner, with differentiation and selection in mind. Although this type of assessment often comes at the end of a course, a year or a school career, the difference lies not so much in the timing as in the intentions of the assessor.

Formative assessment is continuous and often informal. Worksheets are very much a part of formative assessment, affording opportunities for the regular and informal checking of progress and for guidance from the teacher about the tasks in hand.

Diagnostic assessment is an aspect of formative assessment. The purpose of a diagnostic test is to discover if the pupil is encountering difficulties, and the test is conducted during the course/unit, rather than at the end, while there is still time for remedial action.

Norm referenced assessment, which is the traditional type of assessment, measures a pupil relative to others in the group. Its main purpose is to 'sort out' pupils, e.g. ranking, selection, obtaining a class order etc.

Criterion referenced assessment measures performance against a previously determined standard of mastery - that is to say, a pupil's performance is described in terms of what he can do (e.g. he can type forty words per minute without error), rather than in terms of how he compares with others (e.g. he can type faster than Jane or John, but is slower than Chris).

Some of the advantages of criterion referenced assessment over norm referenced assessment are shown in Table 5.

Table 5

Norm referenced	*Criterion referenced*
Used as summative assessment for ranking and selection.	Can be used as formative assessment, as part of the learning experience.
50% of pupils have to be below average. Thus, failure is built into this approach.	The emphasis is on positive statements of what each pupil can do. It is possible for all pupils, if they attain the criteria, to pass.
Pupils do not know what the questions are going to be. At times, a norm referenced exam can be like a conspiracy against the pupil.	The criteria which the pupils have to achieve are clearly laid down and known by the pupils from the start.
There is a strong element of competition and one individual trying to do better than another.	More possibilities for co-operation towards common goals/group work, second drafts etc.
Tests usually summative, coming at the end of the unit or course when it is too late to take remedial action.	There are obvious diagnostic and remedial possibilities with continuous feedback to teacher and pupil on areas of strength and weakness.

Grade related criteria are an attempt to retain the positive characteristics of criterion referenced assessment, while at the same time grading pupils for the purposes of public examinations and certification to meet the requirements of industry, universities etc.

In the Scottish Standard Grade Certificate of Education, grade related criteria are defined as a set of broad indicators or descriptions of expected performance in key aspects of the subject at the different levels of Standard Grade Award.

Examples of these have already been given in Chapter 3. Further examples are given in this chapter in Tables 7 and 8, Example 9 and Case study 9.

In many instances, if you were handed a set of questions, tasks or exercises, you would not be able to tell whether it was a diagnostic, criterion-referenced or norm-referenced test. This is because the difference lies in what happens after the assessment has been made and in what is done with the information gained from the assessment. A test is a diagnostic test if you use it to discover who is having difficulties and what kind of difficulties, and then use that information to take remedial action. Exactly the same test is a norm referenced test if the information is used to put pupils in a rank order. The main difference is in the user's intention.

In many instances, too, if handed this set of questions, tasks or exercises you might find it difficult to say whether it was a revising or summarizing worksheet or a test. All worksheets are informal assessments since they provide you with information about the pupil, about his progress, his strengths and weaknesses, his pace of working, his level of motivation etc. What makes it a formal test is, again, a decision on your part that this is what your intention is and the fact that you might record the results for use by other people.

Assessment of core work

The intention of the assessment at the end of the core is not to place pupils in rank order or gain a spread of marks. For all the pupils to show complete mastery of the core material is highly desirable (though unlikely). The assessment is based on the core objectives which have been made known to the pupils. The assessment should be regarded as part of the learning process of the unit.

The purpose of the assessment is first to discover whether a pupil has mastered the objectives of this core. Usually a mark of about 85 per cent is taken as evidence of mastery. Remember that those who complete the core the fastest are not always the high achievers. Being first to finish does not always mean the objectives have been mastered.

What is considered as a satisfactory 'pass mark' will vary from one subject to another. In a linear subject like Maths, where one step must be understood before the next one can be tackled, the mastery level needs to be higher than in a subject where the same concepts, ideas or words will crop up again in a different unit (English, for example).

The second purpose is to discover which pupils need remedial help and reinforcement (those below 85 per cent) and which are ready to proceed to extension work (those above this percentage).

In some cases, lack of mastery may indicate haste, carelessness or absence, rather than genuine difficulty with the work. In these instances a straight return to the core (or the relevant section of it) would be sufficient.

KEY: / = Core not completed

c = Core completed

© = Core completed after remedial help

E = Extension work completed

Pupil's name	Progress through units			
	Unit one	Unit two	Unit three	Unit four
Robert	CE	CE	CE	CE
David	©	/	©	©
Thomas	C	C	C	CE
Graham	/	/	/	©
Irene	C	C	C	C
Amy	©	C	C	CE
Patricia	©	©	©	C
Sally	C	C	CE	CE

Figure 24 *Typical progress chart*

Sometimes it is possible to design your test or worksheet so that not only does it tell you who is having difficulty, but also what the nature of the difficulty is (see Case studies 6 and 7).

Since pupils are working at their own pace they will be taking the test at different times. Once pupils understand the system and know that they cannot proceed beyond the core until they have mastered it, they usually do not ask to take the test until they know they are ready for it.

Sometimes a bottleneck in marking the core test develops. Some teachers overcome this by using self-marking schemes. Pupils apply for the answer sheet on completing the test (or it is pinned on the wall). If the answer is open-ended or a matter of opinion, the answer sheet, at that point, says 'see the teacher'. It helps if you can use objective tests which can be marked by overlaying a grid or transparency (see example 8). In some instances a formal test is not needed. If the teacher is able to observe how each pupil copes with the worksheets and move round the class giving individual attention, this may provide sufficient information on progress and the difficulties arising. There is scope, too, for self-assessment by the pupil (not the same as self-marking – see Example 7).

The main point about the assessment, whether formal or informal, is that it comes at a stage in the unit when there is still time to take remedial action to help those who are having difficulties, and still time to give the fliers their wings. A test at the end of a unit comes too late to do anything.

In whatever way you assess progress with these different levels of worksheets, it is important to keep a record. Figure 24 gives a simple system.

Teachers sometimes ask: 'How do you have an end-of-term exam if they haven't all done the same work? And how can you give grades on a report card?'

An end-of-term examination should not be necessary if continuous assessment has been employed. One possibility for grades and reports is shown in Figure 25. It is more informative to give a grade for each unit, rather than an overall grade. The wider the range of activity covered by a single grade or mark, the more inscrutable and meaningless it becomes.

First Year Pupil Report   Subject: Geography

Class: 1C   Name of Pupil: Amy

Classwork		
Unit 1	Mapwork	C
Unit 2	Home Area	B
Unit 3	Weather	B
Unit 4	Farming	A

Explanation of letters used

A. Pupil has successfully completed all the main work in this part, plus the extra work.

B. Pupil has completed all the main work in this part, plus some of the extra work.

C. Pupil has managed to complete all the main work after extra help and revision.

D. Pupil has not managed to complete all the main work in this part despite extra help and revision.

Figure 25 *Typical report with grades*

Case study 6

This study concerns the fixing of a position on a map grid with a six-figure reference. For those of you who have forgotten how they work, the grid reference for the dot in square P in Figure 26 is 178602. In this reference, the 17 and 60 fix the position of the main square, and the 8 and 2 fix the position within the square.

As I have already said, the correct answer is (iii). The alternatives (known as the 'distractors') of this multi-choice question are not simply picked at random; they reflect the most common misunderstandings which pupils have when trying to master grid references. Thus (i) is the reference a pupil would arrive at if he read the figure along the side *before* he had read the figures along the top; (ii) is the reference a pupil would arrive at if he used the higher rather than the lower number bordering the square; and (iv) is the reference a pupil would arrive at if, when fixing the position within the square (the third and sixth figures), he confused the horizontal and vertical readings.

Exercises

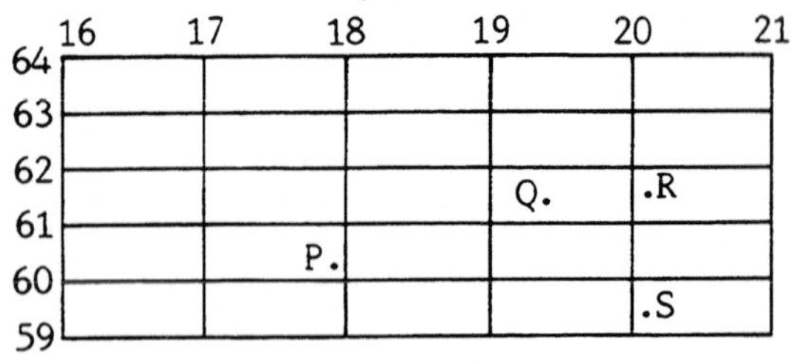

	16–17	17–18	18–19	19–20	20–21
64–63					
63–62					
62–61				Q.	.R
61–60		P.			
60–59					.S

Which is the correct 6 figure grid-reference for the dot in Square P?

(i) 602178

(ii) 618182

(iii) 178602

(iv) 608178

Figure 26 *Case study 6*

Constructing a worksheet, exercise or test in this manner helps you to diagnose where the pupil is going wrong and therefore take the appropriate remedial action. One answer, of course, would not be sufficient evidence; but if in squares Q, R and S the same type of mistake was repeated, you would know not only that this pupil was having difficulty, but what the cause of the difficulty was.

Case study 7

In this study the same question is asked in three different ways. In version A the aim of the question is not diagnostic. In B and C we see differing structures each aimed at revealing where the pupil is experiencing difficulties.

Version A

The teacher has set a norm referenced test with the questions increasing in complexity (Figure 27(a)). He might expect his most able pupils to do all of them correctly. The teacher is concerned with obtaining an end-of-course or end-of-term mark to use for ranking and selection purposes, and not with diagnosing the type of error which his pupils are making, and so he has simply given a mark without indicating why the answer was wrong.

Version B

In this question the purpose is to diagnose at what stage in the calculation the pupil is going wrong. A structured question has been used, breaking the question down into the essential stages. The teacher has written his comments on the sheet.

Using the information provided, make the following tidal predictions (tide tables are provided).

1. The time of a.m. high water at Oban on 1st August. ....
11·50 ✓ 2
2. The time of p.m. low water at Oban on 4th August. ....
8·46 ✓ 2
3. The time of afternoon low water at Loch Beag on 10th August. ....
15·03 ✗

4/6

Figure 27(a) *Case study 7 - version A*

1. The tide table shows that morning high tide at Oban on 10th August is .... 7·05 (am) ✓ not needed with a 24 hour clock
2. Adjusting for British Summer Time, this becomes .... 8 05 a.m ✓
3. The time difference between Oban and Loch Beag is .... + 0·58 mins ✗ ✓
4. High tide at Loch Beag is at .... 9·03 (−116 mins)
5. Adjusting to calculate the next low tide by (Adding) ✓ Subtracting .... 6 hours ✓
6. Time of afternoon low tide at Loch Beag on 10th August is .... 15·03 (pm) (−116 mins) ✓

The table tells you to subtract 58 minutes not add which puts your next high tide out by 116 (58×2) minutes.

Figure 27(b) *Case study 7 - version B*

Tick the box which shows the correct time of afternoon low water at Loch Beag on 10th August.

Calculation		Mistake typified by calculation
12.07	☐	(Forgot to adjust for Summer Time).
15.03	☐	(Added time difference from Oban, instead of subtracting).
13.07	☐	(The correct answer).
11.51	☐	(Looked up 10th July instead of 10th August, also misunderstanding of the 24 hour clock).
14.03	☐	(Combination of errors 1 and 2).

Figure 27(c) *Case study 7 - version C*

Although this pupil's calculations are thrown out by his error at stage 3, he has applied the correct principles and therefore the stages are ticked.

Version C

In this exercise or test the purpose is again diagnostic. Instead of choosing the distractors (alternatives) at random, each corresponds to the answer that a pupil will arrive at if he makes certain typical mistakes (Figure 27(c), p. 41).

Of course a pupil may be failing for reasons which are not revealed by the test, or simply through errors in calculation. The teacher may have to sit down with a pupil, and go over several examples on a one-to-one basis to discover where the trouble lies. It sometimes helps to ask the pupil to describe aloud the mental process he is following as he tackles each step.

The next step would be to analyse the results and consider what remedial action is required.

POOR WORLD

Decide, given the information in Table 1, whether the countries A–E shown in Table 2 are most likely to be RICH COUNTRIES or POOR COUNTRIES. Put your answers (ticks) in Table 3.

Table 1

	RICH COUNTRY	POOR COUNTRY
Life expectancy	More than 60 (high)	Less than 60
Number of people per doctor	Less than 2000 (low)	More than 2000 (high)
Food consumption (calories)	More than 2400 (high)	Less than 2400 (high)
Literacy	More than 80% (high)	Less than 80% (low)

Table 2

	LIFE EXPECTANCY	NUMBER OF PEOPLE PER DOCTOR	FOOD CONSUMPTION (calories)	LITERACY (number of people who can read and write)
COUNTRY A	45	6000	1600	28%
COUNTRY B	71	870	3325	99%
COUNTRY C	42	3200	2000	60%
COUNTRY D	65	1200	2600	91%
COUNTRY E	40	17820	2100	58%

Table 3

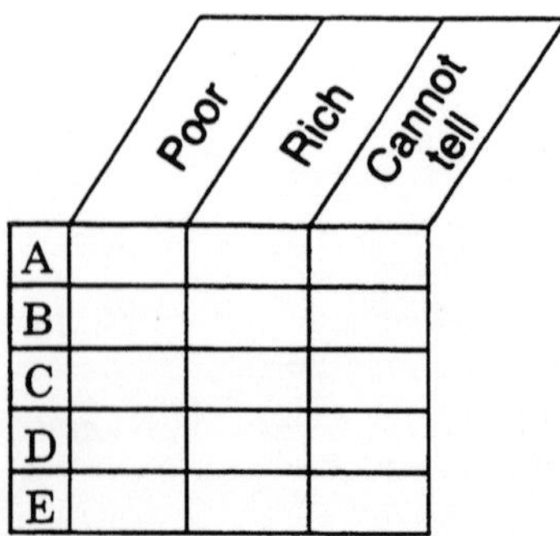

Figure 28 *Example 6*

N O W....

Are you ready for the test? Can you do all the exercises marked?

YES ☐ Ask the teacher for the test-paper and answer it without looking at your notes.

I'M NOT SURE ☐ revise your notes, particularly the exercises marked.

Which parts do you find most difficult? ....

....

....

....

Don't worry. You can do the test a second time and there is a Revision Unit to help you.

Figure 29 *Case study 8*

If a large proportion of the pupils are obviously not grasping a particular stage, it may be that the teacher needs to think about rewording his explanation or altering some other aspect of his teaching method.

Example 6
The example (Figure 28. p. 42) is from *A Diagnostic Resource in Geography* by H.D. Black and R. Goring, Scottish Council for Research in Education, 1983.

Case study 8
The worksheet in the study (Figure 29, p. 43) comes at the end of the core worksheets of a unit for 12-year-old pupils. The intention is to introduce them to the idea of self-assessment and to help them to feel that they are partners with the teacher in their own learning. Certain exercises in the unit are marked with an asterisk. At the start of the unit, pupils are told that the core test will be based on the exercises marked in this way.

The actual test differs by one or two distractors and the choices are listed in a different order. Pupils know this and do not simply try to memorize in which boxes they put the ticks or crosses etc.

It may seem strange to some teachers to tell the pupils in advance what is going to be in their test. But this is the nature of criterion-referenced assessment – its aim is mastery of the desired objectives, and if this is one way of doing it, why not? Of course if you wanted to assess their ability to apply the concepts in a different context or to handle different examples, you couldn't do this. However, this is a first-year mixed-ability course and this approach seems reasonable at this level.

Example 7
The following is an example of a worksheet designed for diagnosis through self-assessment.

MY COMMENTS
The aim of the unit was ....

....

I think I achieved this aim completely/partly/not at all.

When doing this work the difficulties I had were ....

....

....

The things I enjoyed about this work were ....

....

....

..............................Date ....Teacher's initials

Example 8
If multi-choice questions are being used, marking is quicker if pupils are asked to put their answer on an answer grid. In Figure 30 there are questions 1–5, each with a choice of responses A, B, C or D.

The teacher constructs a master grid of exactly the same size on card or acetate sheet. He cuts out the squares from the card which contain the correct answers, or (in the case of the acetate) shades over all but the correct squares. He lays the master grid on top of the pupil's grid. Only the correct answers show through. Thus in the example given above, the teacher would see at a glance that the pupil is correct only on questions 1 and 3.

Worksheets and grade related criteria

In Scotland the 14–16 Standard Grade Examination is based on grade related criteria (GRC). A brief outline of the system might be useful since England and Wales are likely to move

Pupil answer grid

Q	A	B	C	D
1		×		
2				×
3				×
4			×	
5	×			

Teacher master grid

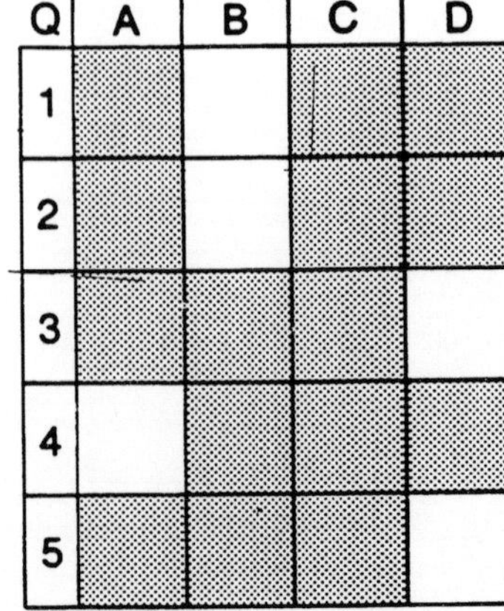

Figure 30 *Example 8*

in the same direction. Details vary from one subject to another, but all subjects have certain features in common.

GRC are broad indicators or descriptions of expected performance in key aspects of a given subject at the three different levels of award (Foundation, General and Credit Levels). They imply, as the name suggests, a move toward criterion referencing. They aim to give positive recognition to pupil achievements, provide challenge for all pupils, identify key aspects of the subject, and supply criteria for internal and external use so that both teachers and the Scottish Examination Board can refer to a common and explicit reference in awarding grades. In summary form they are intended as meaningful resumés of individual achievement, for pupils, parents and employers.

GRC are organized under the broad headings of *assessable elements* (otherwise known as Summary GRC). Table 6 shows the assessable elements for some of the main subjects.

Table 6

English	*Science*	*Maths*	*Contemporary social subjects*
Talking	Handling Information	Interpreting Information	Enquiry
Listening	Knowledge & Understanding	Selecting a Strategy	Knowledge & Understanding
Reading	Problem Solving	Processing Data	Communication
Writing	Practical Skills	Communicating Information	Critical Thinking
		Problem Solving	
		Practical Skills	

Table 7 shows a summary, followed by the extended version, of the GRC for Mathematics, such as would be used on reports and as a resumé for employers. Grade 6 is the lower end of the scale. In some subjects, precise descriptions at every level of the seven-point scale have not yet been laid down.

Table 8 shows how, in Geography, the summary GRC are amplified into Extended GRC, which are the criteria to which teachers work and upon which worksheets would be based.

In Tables 6, 7 and 8 it can be seen that the emphasis is very much upon process and skills rather than on content. In most subjects, broad topics or themes are defined, but these are seen as vehicles for arriving at the fulfilment of the GRC rather than an end in themselves. Often the flexibility, choice and latitude within these broad topics is such that, for the purposes of an external examination, there is little common ground in terms of content covered, and even less common ground at Foundation level which is mainly internally assessed. The unifying factor is the GRC. These are central to the whole system.

Interpreting and Communicating Information
Summary GRC for Grade Points 6 and 5
The pupil is able to interpret mathematical information in forms such as simple tables, scale drawings with scales in words, formulae in words and graphs where the scales are straightforward, assuming the context is familiar.

The pupil is able to communicate mathematical information obtained from a familiar real-life context where the format in which the information is to be communicated is specified and straightforward. The information would be communicated neatly and intelligibly in forms such as bar graphs, simple tables, scale drawings and formulae in words. The pupil is able to describe how he solved a problem in concrete terms.

Table 7

Grade Point 6	*Grade Point 5*
The pupil is able to interpret mathematical information met in familiar real-life contexts.	
The information could be presented in a simple statement, orally or in writing, with numbers expressed in words, or figures, or in more abstract forms such as simple tables which clearly present two categories of data: the pupil is able to	
choose relevant pieces of data from the table.	make 'reverse' use of the table (possibly with further categories).
line graphs with straightforward scales: the pupil is able to	
find, given one value, the corresponding value.	recognize the trend in the graph where there is only one main trend.
bar graphs with straightforward scales: the pupil is able to	
read off the height of a bar level with a numbered division	
interpolate half way between two clearly numbered divisions.	interpolate.
piecharts: the pupil is able to use the relative size of the sectors to find the largest or smallest value.	
pictographs: with whole or halved symbols.	with fractions of symbols.
scale drawings and maps where the scale is expressed in words; mathematical diagrams; simple formulae expressed in words; simple codes.	
flowcharts:	
with one simple decision box.	with two or three decision boxes.

Continued over

straightforward scales on everyday measuring instruments: the pupil is able to read

between which two numbered divisions the pointer lies.	between which two marked divisions the pointer lies.
	between which two numbered divisions on a conversion scale the pointer lies.

The pupil is able to interpret:

the notation used in a mariner's compass - eight main compass points and 3-figure bearings

the notation of decimal fractions and the 24-hour clock.

The pupil is able to recognize familiar three-dimensional shapes from

(i) their two-dimensional representations

(ii) their nets by cutting out and folding if necessary.

The pupil is able to communicate mathematical information obtained from a familiar situation in real-life where the format in which the information is to be communicated is specified and straightforward (i.e. structure of table or scales on graph). The information would be communicated, neatly and intelligibly, by means of a simple statement with numbers expressed in words, or figures, or by

completing (i.e. given the format)	drawing

tables, bar graphs, mathematical diagrams, two-dimensional representations of given simple three-dimensional shapes, maps and scale drawings where the scale is expressed in words.

means of a simple formula expressed in words.

The pupil is able to describe how he solved a problem in concrete terms, i.e. by direct references to specific values in the problem.

Some difficulties encountered in matching worksheets to GRC

Early attempts often reflect the fact that teachers are used to a content-orientated curriculum. Worksheets, at first, tend to emphasize factual knowledge and fail to reflect the new emphasis on process and skills.

The skills and processes which the GRC describe cannot usually be achieved through traditional, didactic methods. The GRC attached to Practical Skills, Handling Information or Enquiry, for example, imply in their wording such approaches as 'hands on' experience, group discussion, role-playing use of source material and media, individual study. In the old style examinations, as long as a teacher covered the syllabus, the methods he used were up to him. Now, certain methodologies built into and part of the GRC, are essential to the skills and processes, and checking that they are present is an important part of the moderation of the curriculum that is presented by each school. Worksheets and the tasks to which they direct pupils have to take account of these methods. Early attempts at worksheets for GRC sometimes try to put new wine into old bottles.

For many subjects the topics or themes for Scotland's new Standard Grade Examination are not very different from the former 'O' grade topics for which teachers already have resources and worksheets. There is a strong temptation, therefore, to use the same worksheets and try to match them up with the new GRC. This seldom works. They are often near the target, but seldom

Table 8

Critical thinking: Geography

	Grade 6	*Grade 5*	*Grade 2*
Summary GRC	The pupil has demonstrated the ability to use straightforward information to draw valid conclusions and to express a valid point of view.	The pupil has demonstrated the ability to use straightforward information to draw valid conclusions and to express and support a valid pont of view.	The pupil has demonstrated the ability to make deductions from a variety of data, develop an argument supported by evidence and express and recognise alternative valid points of view.
Extended GRC	The pupil can demonstrate the ability to 1. make an appropriate deduction from data. 2. give a valid point of view based on a set of straightforward related statements. 3. identify the purpose of, and bias in a simple and straightforward text or photograph or A/V source	In addition, the pupil can demonstrate the ability to 1. make appropriate deductions from simple and related sets of data 2. give and support a valid point of view based on simple data	In addition, the pupil can demonstrate the ability to 1. make appropriate deductions from a wide variety of data 2. express fluently and sustain a valid point of view 3. recognise alternative valid points of view 4. support an argument with evidence 5. draw valid conclusions based on a set of related data 6. analyse a geographical problem in a logical manner

Source: *Experimental Guidelines for Standard Grade Geography at Foundation Level.* Scottish Examination Board, 1984

PRESENT INFORMATION IN WRITTEN FORM, CONVEYING A PURPOSE OR IDEA.

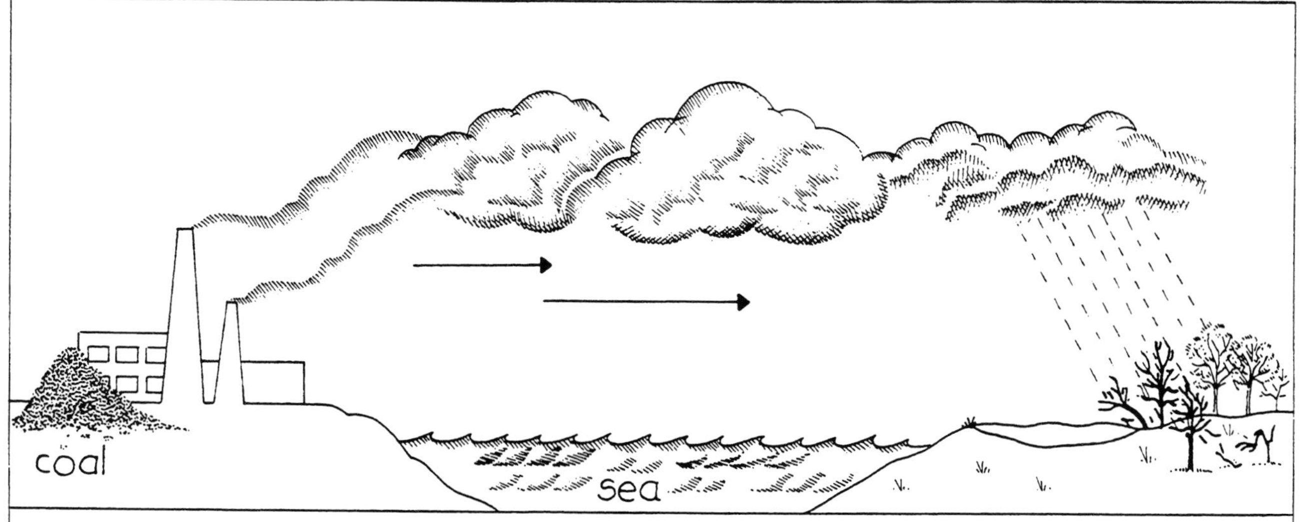

These pictures tell a story of modern pollution.

Write a paragraph to describe this story. Use the words

sulphur, smoke, acid rain, fossil fuel.

Air is polluted with smoke and chemicals. These drawings show three stages in an experiment to measure how dirty the air is around a school.

1. vaseline

vaseline smear

microscope slide

3. slide

microscope

school

2.

outside

Explain, in words, how you would compare the dirt in the air at opposite ends of the school playground.

Figure 31 *Case study 9* Source: *Foundation Item Bank for Science*, Aberdeen College of Education, 1984

MAIN TASK COLLATE RELEVANT INFORMATION FROM SEVERAL GIVEN SIMPLE SOURCES

Here are some birds which are commonly found in different places (habitats).

Woodland - woodpigeon, rook, woodpecker

Hilly region - grouse, eagle, lark

Farmland - pheasant, lark, woodpigeon

Sea shore - gull, eider duck, cormorant

River bank - mallard, kingfisher, dipper

Here is a map of a certain part of the country.

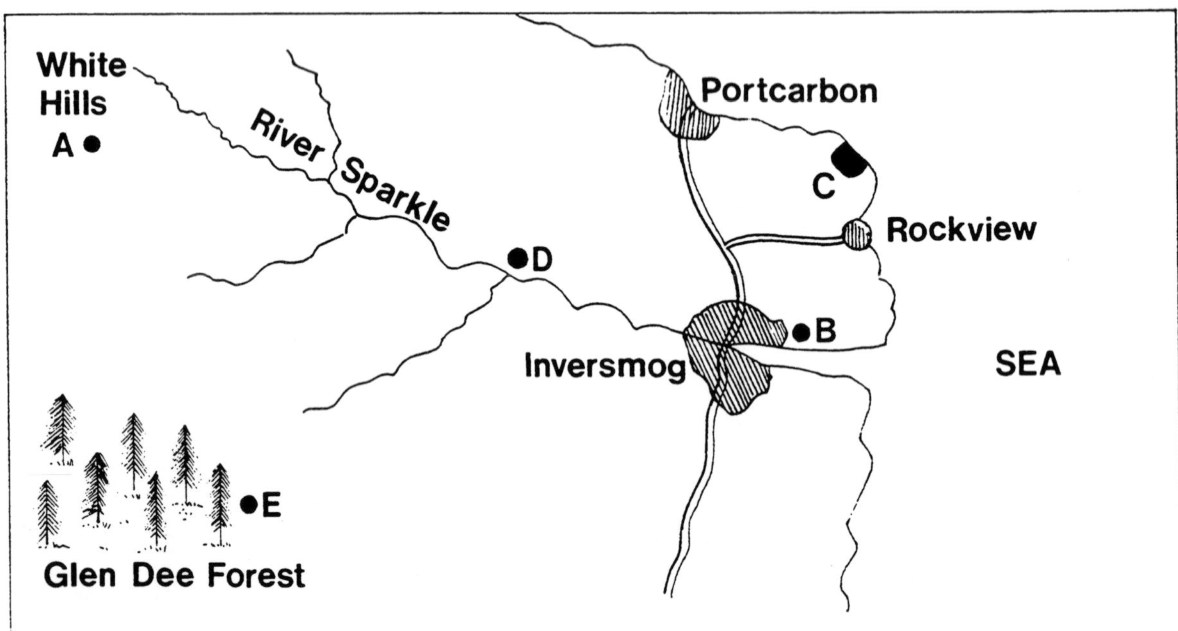

Use the information given to work out where you would go (A,B,C,D or E) to have a good chance of seeing a

(a) woodpecker

(b) eagle

(c) dipper

(d) cormorant

Figure 32 Case study 9 Source: *Foundation Item Bank for Science*, Aberdeen College of Education, 1984 hit the bullseye; the required methodology may not be built in; there is seldom an even balance between all the required GRC. The starting point has to be the GRC, and questions such as: 'What learning experiences do we need to devise that will help the pupil to achieve this GRC?' and 'What will give him an opportunity to display this skill at a higher grade of performance if he has the capability?'

Example 9 from *Guidelines for Contemporary Social Studies at Foundation and General Levels* (Scottish Examination Board, 1984) shows the grade related criteria for one of the Enquiry skills and the sort of pupil performance expected and towards which worksheets might direct pupils.

Case study 9 shows the match between certain GRC for Science and the worksheets that were specifically designed to help pupils achieve them. See Figures 31 and 32, previous two pages.

Case study 9

At the Foundation level of the Standard Grade, internal assessment plays a large part. A difficulty encountered by teachers is deciding what counts as evidence of a performance level having been attained and what place a completed worksheet has as part of this evidence. The next section on folio assessment looks at some of the possibilities.

Example 9

Purpose
E2 to find and extract relevant information from a source.

Extended GRC	*Performance examples*
Grade 6 The candidate has demonstrated ability:	
(a) to obtain specified information from a printed source;	Obtain details of the basic weekly pay and hours worked for a named job by referring to a given job advertisement.
(b) to use a system of coordinates (up to four figures) to find specified information;	Use a four-figure reference to find the name of a village in a grid square.
(c) to use a map/diagram and its key to find specified information;	On a tourist map of a town, locate the railway station/ library/police station.
(d) to obtain specified information from - a visual source - a spoken source - an audio-visual source	After a talk from the local police, name the most common crimes in the area; from 2 slides of a town in the 17th and 20th centuries, list major environmental changes which have taken place.
(e) to obtain specified information from a field source by observing and by listening.	As a result of a visit to a local firm, obtain information about working conditions there.
Grade 5 *In addition*, the candidate has demonstrated ability:	
(a) to obtain specified information within a limited range of relevant printed sources using a simple reference system or index;	Obtain details of the basic weekly pay and conditions for a number of named jobs by reference to a page of job advertisements in alphabetical order in a local newspaper.
(b) to use maps/diagrams to obtain specified information;	Use four-figure map references to acquire information from a 1:50 000 map on the comparative sizes of two settlements.
(c) to obtain specified information from a limited combination of visual sources, spoken sources and audio-visual sources;	After viewing a video on Northern Ireland, provide examples of violent acts carried out by both sides.
(d) to obtain specified information from a limited range of field sources by observing and listening.	Obtain information about the working conditions in three different local firms by visiting them and interviewing employees.

Worksheets and folio assessment

The pupil builds up a folio of finished work, from which the best (say) six out of twelve are presented for final assessment. The work might include the pupil's own essays, short stories, poems, magazine articles, taped oral work, with a record of reading etc. (English); or maps, histograms, records of fieldwork (Geography), drawings, paintings, collages, photographs (Art) etc., and completed worksheets.

The work submitted is not necessarily an unaided first draft as might be produced under examination conditions, where the time is limited and there is no access to reference materials. Redrafting, after discussion with the teacher, encourages a high standard of work, and it is valid to assess not only the pupil's raw work, but also his ability to learn to achieve, his responsiveness to encouragement and criticism, his ability to review his work critically, to improve, to develop presentational skills etc.

The act of selecting the contents of the folio, of discussing it with the teacher and deciding why one piece of work is better than another, is in itself a learning experience.

In assembling a selection of his or her best work, a pupil has to be aware of the assessable element that is being assessed in any piece of work. This, also, is a learning experience, focusing the pupil's attention on the desired skills. As a form of continuous assessment it helps to motivate pupils by showing them that all their course work is relevant.

Example 10

Record of pupil work
This sheet should be attached to the folder containing the pupil's work, and be completed by the teacher when the item is put in the folder. Where a piece of resource material is used, a copy of this (if possible) should be included in the folder, e.g. map, photograph.

Name: J. Smith
Class: 4F
School: Dumbiedykes Academy

Date of entry in folder	*Topic/related theme*	*Brief description of item of pupil work*	*Elements being assessed*	*Grade given*
15.9.84	Leisure & recreation	Completion of table of map information of available	Enquiry	6
		leisure & recreation facilities in given section of 1:50 000 OS map (key given)	Handling information	5
19.11.84	Landscape studies	Multiple choice test of 10 items given in class to test understanding of Key Ideas (v) 'The Countryside provides raw materials'	Knowledge and understanding	5
23.1.85	Landscape studies	Given an oblique black and white air photograph and a set of questions, the pupil was asked to suggest why certain land-uses were in evidence	Critical thinking	6

(Source: *Standard Grade Geography: Experimental Guidelines for Foundation Level*, Scottish Examination Board, 1984)

Chapter Six

Language matters

We have a suspected CVA, so we need to do an electroencephalogram. On the other hand, if the salpingo-oophorectomy was too late, it could be mets.

Unless you are a doctor or a nurse you probably had only a vague idea what this passage meant. You can make a few guesses and deductions (which may be erroneous), but mostly it is incomprehensible – as incomprehensible as some of our worksheets and allied textbooks are to our less able pupils.

With the Bullock Report *A Language for Life* (DES, 1975) came the recommendation that awareness of pupils' language development and language problems was relevant to all subjects and all teachers. It is through language that children learn. They learn through what you, the teacher, say, through the language of worksheets and textbooks, through their own writing and talking.

Case study 10 is placed immediately after this introductory section to illustrate how easy it is to be unaware that what appears to be a straightforward piece of prose can be causing all sorts of difficulties and misunderstandings.

The first part of this chapter considers talking and writing as pupil activities generated by worksheets. The second part of the chapter looks into various formulae for predicting readability, their uses and limitations and their application to texts and worksheets.

Case study 10

The prose passage in Figure 33 was prepared by a teacher for a unit on 'Change'. She then gave it to a Remedial Specialist for comment.

The Remedial Specialist used the material with a class of 15-year-olds, with reading and comprehension ages ranging from 8.6 to 13.6. He read the passage out to the class. He selected some of the more difficult reading/comprehension words in the passage and wrote them on the board. The pupils then underlined them in their worksheet.

The pupils then wrote down the underlined words in a column, and what they thought they meant. The words 'lack', 'area', 'rebuild', 'permission' and 'suitable' were understood by all nine pupils in the group. The word 'refer' was not known and was left blank by all the pupils. A variety of meanings were attributed to the other words; see Table 9 overleaf.

The Remedial Specialist was of the opinion that, even with explanations given, too many new words were being introduced at once in this passage.

Language activities generated by worksheets

The first point to make is that, over a course or a unit as a whole, there should be a balance between talking, listening, reading and writing, that

Changing a Town Boundary

The old part of our town is becoming congested. New roads are needed. Many of the houses are old and beyond repair. There is a lack of open spaces for recreation.

Before this area can be rebuilt the people living there will have to be rehoused.

There is no room within the present city limits so the Council have been given permission by the Government to get an area outside the present area of the town.

Refer to the areas A, B, C and D on the map and study the summary reports on them. You have to decide which area is most suitable for development.

Figure 33 *Case study 10*

Table 9 What the pupils thought the words meant

Word	*Pupil A*	*B*	*C*	*D*	*E*	*F*	*G*	*H*	*I*
Congested	Re-Modernized	Old	Demolished	Renewed	Renewed	Rebuilt	Repaired	Taken down	Re-Modernized
Beyond repair	Needs Repair	Can't repair it	Needing repair	Past the place	On repair	Far away	From one point to another	Can't be repaired	Must be repaired
Recreation	-	-	Needing built	Needs houses	Starting again	-	-	Not enough land	buildings
Rehouse	Redecorate	Move to another house	Move to another house	-	decorate	made into a house	get a new house	get another house	get another house
City limits	Boundary	Boundary	Rules	-	When the city can take no more	Boundary	-	You can only go so far	Boundary
Council	Keep things tidy	-	lot of people deciding things	-	To help people who are poor	to get permission	the people who lend houses	people who own the area	A group who give houses to the poor
Summary report	To report something	-	-	-	-	a paper with information	Report on accident	You get one at end of of term	Tells you whether you are right or wrong.

Source: Bearsden Academy, Glasgow

worksheets have a part to play in maintaining this balance, and by no means need be confined to written language.

Figure 34 is an example of a matrix which can be used to check whether some language aspects are being neglected or others over-emphasized. You may not have time to analyse every worksheet in this way, but it can be a revealing exercise and helps to create a mental checklist for future use.

Pupil talk

Speech is the primary instrument of thought and the process of 'thinking out loud' or 'talking one's way through an idea' is essential to learning. Pupils will not learn merely by taking notes. They must engage, orally, in the language of the subject if they are to grasp its concepts.

> While many teachers recognize that their aim is to initiate a student in a particular mode of analysis, they rarely recognize the linguistic implication of doing so. They do not recognize, in short, that the mental processes they seek to foster are the outcome of a development that originates in speech. A person's impulse to talk over a problem that his thinking has failed to solve is a natural one. (Bullock 12.4)

Does the whole strategy and context within which you use your worksheets encourage task-related talk? What are the seating arrangements while pupils do their worksheets? Have you deliberately created opportunities for talk in the types of task you set in your worksheets (e.g. practical activities in pairs, pairing off for interviews, quizzes, revision tests)? Do you ever use worksheets as preparation and build-up for group discussion? Do you give pupils an opportunity to record some of their work on tape or to explain or demonstrate to others what they have been doing? To what extent do you engage in individual or small group discussion with your pupils while they are working?

Pupil writing

The term 'transactional writing' is generally used to refer to formal prose which is used in an impersonal way to convey information, instructions etc. The term 'expressive writing' refers to writing which allows the writer greater freedom to express thoughts, opinions, feelings, personality and style.

Table 10

Bullock Report Survey: Different Functions of Writing by Subject (% of all writing done in the schools surveyed)

	English	*History*	*Geography*	*RE*	*Science*
Transactional	34	88	88	57	92
Expressive	11	0	0	11	0
Poetic	39	2	0	12	0
Miscellaneous	26	10	12	20	8

Table 10 shows the findings of the Bullock Report survey of the frequency with which these and other types of writing were used in schools. It can be seen that transactional writing is by far the most common type of writing we ask our pupils to do, whereas expressive writing in some subjects

Name of course ______________

						Units/sub-units	
						Small-group discussion	TALKING
						Whole-class discussion	
						Drama/simulations	
						Interviews (taped or real)	
						Informal conversation concerning topic	
						Oral element in assessment	
						Any other	
						Teacher-produced material	READING
						Textbooks	
						Library sources	
						Newspapers, pamphlets, etc.	
						Any other	
						To teacher	LISTENING
						To each other	
						Radio, TV, tapes etc.	
						Songs	
						Any other	
						Note-taking - copied	WRITING
						Note-taking - own notes	
						Worksheets - closed question	
						Worksheets - open-ended question	
						Narrative/imaginative	
						Letter/newspaper article etc.	
						Formal report	
						Any other	

Figure 34 *Curriculum design: language matrix*

hardly occurs at all. And yet there is growing evidence to show that expressive writing is the soil from which transactional writing grows; that through expressive writing a second-hand experience gained from books or lectures can move closer to a first-hand experience. Two quotes will serve to reinforce this important point:

We believe that expressive writing shares some of the virtues of expressive talk in helping a pupil to find his way into a subject. Moreover, it is an important stage in the way to a range of differentiated kinds of writing. (Bullock 12.6)

Theory and practice suggest that if a learner at any level is able to make his own formulations of what he is learning, this is more valuable to him than taking over someone else's pre-formulated language. In practice, this means that pupils often need to have the opportunity to say or write things in their own ways, in their own styles, rather than copying from books or taking notes from dictation. (*Language across the Curriculum: Guidelines for Schools* by M. Marland *et al.*, Heinemann, 1977.)

Another finding of the Bullock Report was that the audience for about half of all secondary school writing was the teacher in his role of examiner and giver of marks. Other types of possible audience for the writer to aim at - such as teacher in his role as trusted adult, the peer group or the public - were neglected. Worksheets can help provide a variety of writing purposes linked to a variety of audiences, so that pupils are given an opportunity to express their thoughts on paper in a variety of ways.

The following two extracts from a document produced by the Education for Industrial Society Project (Scottish Consultative Committee on the Curriculum, 1980), sum up much of this.

Extract A

The problem presents itself at its simplest when colleagues complain that the English Department does not provide them with pupils who can spell and punctuate correctly and write grammatically. Every English teacher needs to be alert to his responsibilities in this area, and should frequently ask himself whether his practice fully exploits the evident desire of the very great majority of pupils to succeed in school work, and, as a necessary step towards that, to achieve competence in the conventions of written English. He should be ready as well, however, to argue that these skills are the concern of every department in the school, and are best developed in context as the need arises. The procedures of an English classroom and the English teacher's awareness of the part played by language in how a child learns in any subject can make an important contribution to the quality of education in the school.

These procedures might be represented as having four stages:

(i) exploration (as when one makes an out-of-school visit, looks at a picture or reads a text);
(ii) oral discussion, at first descriptive, but gradually moving to more analytical and evaluative levels;
(iii) tentative, often informal, written expression;
(iv) formal written statement, incorporating abstract thinking, generalizations, evaluations, conclusions.

This is not, of course, a formula for structuring every lesson. It merely presents in schematic form the English teacher's method.

To appreciate the advantages of the method we must understand the truly creative function of language, that is, that in generating our own language, we are creating our own understanding. Language is the tool which we use to prise open experience so that we may explore it; and, as the exploration proceeds, it is through language that we assess and reassess the experience, reaching new adjustments to it formulated in new language - language, that is, which is new to us.

Many teachers of other subjects know this and are adjusting their methods accordingly. Some of the best language acquisition in a school may be going on in a Physics course where everything is verbally explored. In History classes the imaginative involvement of pupils in historical situations is often achieved through role-playing and creative writing. In Modern Studies, investigation of problems like traffic-flow, with subsequent discussion of the observed facts and the writing up of them, leads to the development of powers of thought and expression in exactly those ways which the CCE Bulletins commend.

On the other hand, some teachers (including some English teachers) are still using methods which involve leaping from stage (i) to stage (iv). This happens when notes are copied from the blackboard or when, in some other fashion, the teacher does all the creative verbalizing himself and the pupil is asked merely to learn the teacher's words. Closed questions which narrow the opportunity for developing responses may also effectively preclude any true generation of language by the pupil.

Extract B

(c) *Writing*

(i) Writing gives form to thinking and therefore is essential to all educational development.
(ii) Pupils leaving school ought to be capable of writing to a standard which at least includes the ability to cope with application forms and letters of application, to make simple reports and keep records. Personal writing, though not much indulged in after school by many pupils, is a vital aspect of writing in school because it reveals the progress and degree of development of ideas. Awareness of the place of different modes of writing and their appropriateness to differing contexts should be a further aspect of the writing ability which pupils should take with them into the world of work.
(iii) There is evidence that not enough writing is being done in schools. Too often what little writing is done in many subject departments is of the one-word answer or multiple-choice type, or involves unthinking copying out of other people's writings.
(iv) Practice is the only way in which writing skills will develop. The teacher must provide appropriate contexts or experiences and let the pupils explore these through writing. In this way young people will learn to use writing experimentally and instrumentally.
(v) Teachers must provide positive help to young leavers through such techniques as drafting and redrafting. This provides constant feedback from the page to the mind of the young writer and vice-versa.

The third extract, although directed at English teachers, is sound advice for all teachers whose worksheets and their related tasks demand any form of extended writing from their pupils - especially if they are slow learners.

Extract C

There should be nothing unfamiliar to any of us about the [illustrated] order of events in the production of a piece of writing. It is the process we all go through when, for example, we write to complain about the bungling of our tax-code. What surprises us, perhaps, when we see it laid out like that, is how many stages of the process actually precede the final copy. Even if we admit that some of the stages, for example, the talking and listening, may take the form of a purely internal debate with ourselves, they must be gone through if the final product is to be of sufficient quality to achieve its purpose.

It is in fact what happens at any time when we attempt to express ourselves through the written word; and applies indeed to occasions when we have to express ourselves in speech with greater care than usual. But because as English teachers we are gifted linguistically, we have found that *our* difficulties arise once we are already half-way up the mountain, at the drafting stage; and our mistake as teachers is that we take the lower slopes for granted, refusing to believe that anyone can be in difficulties there. Because we have been good at writing, it has never been difficult to motivate us towards a repetition of success; because we have had immediate access to vocabulary and a range of syntactical structures, we have had no difficulty in formulating ideas inside our head; because we could visualize the order in which to put our ideas we spent little time in reflection or in making preliminary notes. But very many pupils (by no means just slow learners) find their sticking points precisely at one or more of these early stages of the climb. And this paper is arguing that by attending sympathetically to these stages, the teacher can greatly improve the pupil's ability to communicate in writing - no matter what his level of ability seemingly is. It is arguing, further, that we should deliberately teach all children how to negotiate the succeeding stages of this climb as a *routine* method of learning, of going about *all* written work.

The approach suggested has evolved over the course of six years out of attempts to deal with the difficulties experienced by slower learners in written language. It at once meets the needs of pupils who, having experienced only failure in the past, no longer wish to perform tasks requiring writing; and those who are clever enough to be already, like ourselves, internalizing some stages of the process set out above. It is especially useful therefore in a mixed-ability class.

It makes one assumption: that if we are going to improve a pupil's writing we have to start from the writer's present performance and build gradually on that - NOT set up the criteria of attainment against which his performance is constantly measured.

By doing this we not only encourage children to find writing enjoyable, but actually improve their skills at a speed they can cope with. (*From Speech to Writing* by R. Binns, Scottish Curriculum Development Service, 1978).

Case study 11

This is an example of expressive writing from a science topic for 12-year-olds. As extra language work at the end of the activity sheets, pupils were asked to describe the day's experiment in a letter to a friend. David clearly believes that his own feelings, and incidental information such as the teacher's name, are as interesting to his reader as the experimental details (Figure 35 overleaf).

The source is *Worksheets and School Learning* by R. Beavis and Colin Weatherley (Scottish Council for Educational Technology, Occasional Paper 8, 1980).

Predicting readability levels

Research has shown that individual teachers will vary by up to six or seven years in their estimates of the age at which an average reader can read a particular passage with understanding. It is with good reason, therefore, that the Bullock Report states:

A particularly important teaching skill is that of assessing the difficulty level of books by applying measures of readability. The teacher who can do this is in a better position to match children to reading materials that answer their needs.

Readability formulae, however, have their

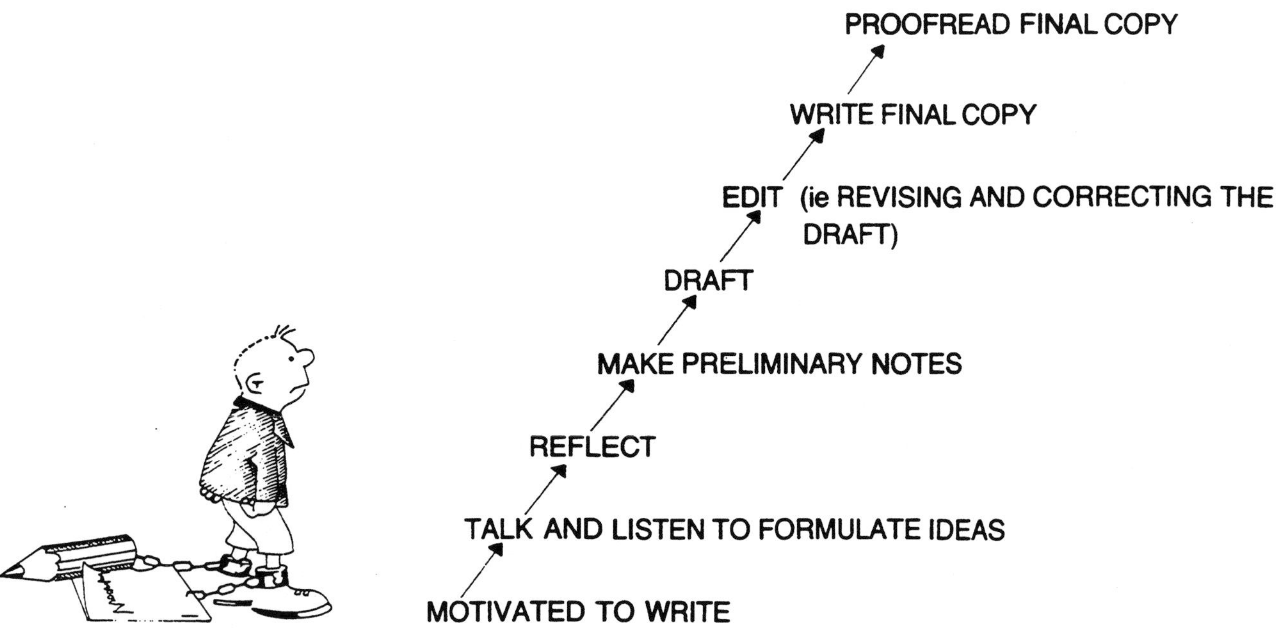

Dear David,

At science today we
had an experment today it
was about energy it was very exciting.
Out teacher is Mr Weatherley. The
experiment was about custard
powder and a candle. First you get
a tin with a tight fitting lid ~~[crossed out]~~, then
a tube going into the side of the
tin, ~~[crossed out]~~ you put some powder
in, light the candle place the
lid on tight, Blow through the
tube, pinch it tight, then Kapow!
off shoots the lid followed by a
flame (~~flame~~) about 50cm's (1½ foot)
high. Then we wrote a quiz
on the board. Then we got
our books home about what
I am writing now.

your's
Sincerely
DAVID
PAXTON.

PS HOW are your experiments getting on.

Figure 35 *Case study 11*

	Validity	Age level accuracy (8–16 age-range)	Ease of application
Flesch formula (Grade score)	●●●●	●●●	●●
Fry graph	●●●●	●●●	●●●
Powers–Summer–Kearl formula	●●●●	●	●●●
Mugford formula and chart	●●●●	●●●●	●●
FOG formula	●●●	●●	●●●●
SMOG formula	●●●	●●	●●●●●
Dale–Chall formula	●●●●●	●●●●	●
Spache formula	●●●●	●●	●●
FORCAST formula	●●	●●	●●●●

Figure 36 *Readability measures - their ease of application* (*source: Readability in the Classroom* by Colin Harrison, 1980)

limitations. No formula yet devised is equally effective throughout the school age range, and some are very time-consuming to apply. Figure 36 summarizes research data on nine readability measures and rates their ease of application.

There are also microcomputer programmes which will calculate the reading level of any text you type in. For example, *Textgrader* (Hutchinson Software, 1982) will calculate the reading level from a choice of seven different formulae.

The Fry Graph

This method is described here because it is one of the most straightforward ways of obtaining a readability index; because, of all the formulae, it retains its accuracy over the widest age range; because it is one of the most reliable and valid measures outside the complicated systems which use pre-selected word lists.

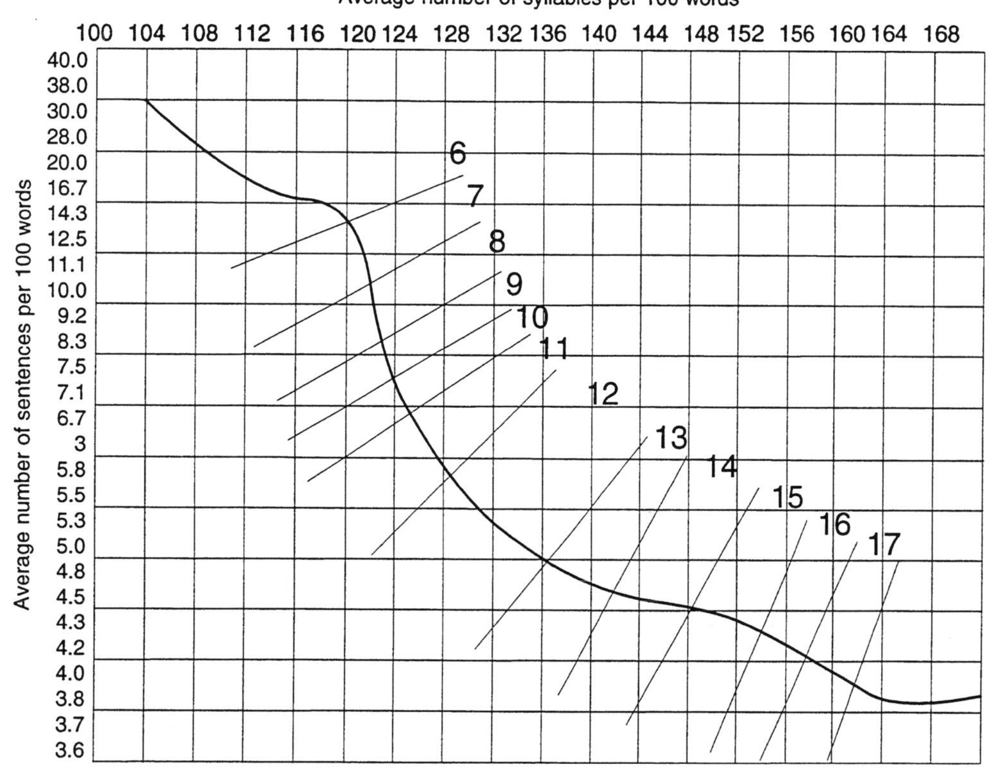

Figure 37 *The Fry Graph*

The method is as follows:

1 Select three separate 100-word passages, preferably at the beginning, middle and end of the material.
2 In each passage find the total number of syllables and the total number of sentences.
3 Average out the number of syllables and sentences for all three passages.
4 Read off on the graph (Figure 37). The nearer to the black line, the more accurate the figure.

The first 100 words of the single passage in Figure 38 have been worked using this formula. The reading age is 10½ approximately, as given by Figure 37.

When counting syllables for numerals and abbreviations, count one syllable for each symbol. For example 1588 has four syllables, HMS has three syllables, & has one syllable.

Readability formulae should be used with critical caution rather than with blind faith. It is as well to remember that they predict rather than measure text difficulty and there is never a perfect correlation between factors such as length of word or sentence and the actual difficulty of a passage of prose. It does not follow that, because a passage is easy to read, it is easy to understand. Passages can contain difficult concepts expressed in simple English.

Other factors influence difficulty - for example, the size of the print; the layout of the page; whether or not there are illustrations; whether the 'difficult' polysyllabic words are, in fact, well known names; the frequency of certain words.

Instructional and independent reading levels are different. At secondary level, children can usually cope with texts up to two years above their own reading age if given help and support. A highly motivated child can cope with a text well above his accepted level. Never use a formula to deny access to what a child positively wants to read.

In subjects such as Mathematics and Science where the prose is often highly compressed and very concise, readability scores are likely to be below the 'true' difficulty level. Also, some Science textbooks or information sheets have such a high content of symbolic as opposed to verbal language that it is questionable whether they can be meaningfully subjected to readability analysis.

The Cloze procedure

The Cloze procedure is a way of testing comprehension. The tester deletes words from a passage on a regular basis. He then uses the number of correctly guessed words as an index of how much the reader has understood. Using the Cloze procedure has the advantage that we can measure the pupils against the text and the text against the pupils without the intervention of somebody else's arithmetic.

Taking the newspaper article about Liverpool which we used with the Fry Graph, the passage would look like this:

Liverpool, __________ title favourites, are back to their best and top __________ the League again, at long last!

It's not the Anfield __________ blowing their own trumpet, the compliment comes from __________ stunned Manchester City Boss, Tony Brook. He said '__________ were right back to their best today and when __________ are on song there is no one to touch __________.'

Poor Tony must dread going to Liverpool. Last season __________ crashed 4–0 and it would have been the __________ score this time but for the last minute goal __________ Colin Bell.

In this case, because there are ten blanks, multiply by ten to obtain a percentage score. A Cloze score of 40 – 45 per cent correct answers seems to indicate an acceptable level of

Book sings the praises of Liverpool

By MIKE ELLIS

Liverpool 4, Man. C. 1

LIVERPOOL, the title favourites, are back to their best and top of the League again — at long last!

It's not the Anfield camp blowing their own trumpet — the compliment comes from a stunned Manchester City boss, Tony Book.

He said: "Liverpool were right back to their best today and when they are on song there is no-one to touch them."

Poor Tony must dread going to Liverpool. Last season City crashed 4–0 and it would have been the same score this time but for a last-minute goal from Colin Bell.

It was the "Old Guard" who delivered the goods.

Brian Hall, reclaiming his place from £170,000 signing Terry McDermott, celebrated with two goals and John Toshack, who is keeping £200,000 Ray Kennedy on the sidelines maintained his goal-a-game average since his move to Leicester broke down.

Steve Heighway, showing a welcome return to form, scored the other.

Creaky

City did not know what hit them and their creaky defence was in danger of total collapse. Only the industrious Doyle and Corrigan spared them from a worse thrashing.

Figure 38 *Passage for application of the Fry Graph*

comprehension for texts used at an instructional level. For texts used for independent reading, 60 per cent correct answers would seem to be more appropriate.

In applying the Cloze procedure, the following rules should pertain:

- Start at least one word in from the beginning of your selected passage.
- Words are deleted from the text on a strict arithmetical basis, every tenth word being most useful for school use. The strict arithmetical rule is broken only if it will remove a word essential to the context. For example, in the passage just used, the third blank should have been 'Anfield'; but a place name cannot be deduced by logic (unless it has occurred before in the passage), so in this case the eleventh word was deleted.
- Pupils must supply the missing words without benefit of clues or lists of words to choose from. The blank spaces should all be of the same size and not correlate with the length of the missing word.
- The exact word must be supplied and not a synonym. For example, in the last blank space, the word must be 'from' - 'by' cannot be accepted as correct.
- There is no time limit.

The nature of the information in the passage can influence the ease or difficulty of filling the gaps. They are generally much harder to fill in a technical, mathematical or scientific text where specialized words with specific meanings are used which may not lend themselves to guesswork.

The teacher must use professional judgement about when the Cloze procedure can or cannot be used.

Teachers' judgements

Whilst readability ratings by individual teachers are unreliable, pooled judgements by groups of teachers have been found to be more accurate than even the best formulae. Organizing such groups and agreeing on a common verdict, however, would score low on the ease of application rating in Figure 34. The professional expertise of teachers, however, should be taken account of. Reading formulae and Cloze procedures are intended to complement a teacher's judgement and experience rather than supersede it. Readability formulae, for instance, cannot assess the literary value of a book, nor can they assess a child's interests or emotional needs. One thing which no formula can measure is what experience a child brings to any reading task - you are best placed to know that.

Some teachers may claim that they make their evaluation by instinct or 'gut-feeling' based on experience. But more teachers are more likely to be right more of the time if we can identify some of the ingredients of such judgements. Some of the factors involved would seem to be:

- Is it free of 'noise'? Is the information you want the pupil to reach clearly obtainable - not cluttered by distracting parentheses or irrelevant extra information? Is there a clear pattern to which you can direct the child's attention, e.g. a sequence of events, comparison and contrast, statements followed by supporting information etc?
- Is it within the child's experience - or at any rate close enough to it that a little thought will take him from the stage he is at to the next one? Has the child got enough experience to cope with what is in the text? Has he been led up to this point so that what he now reads is something he can join on to what he knows, or is he required to make some impossible leap? Is his progress blocked by some piece of knowledge beyond his reach?
- Is the language arrangement as straightforward as it might be? This operates at both vocabulary and structural level. Does the author use vocabulary within the experiences of the child's years? Does he use long sentences including many subordinate clauses, or overload his nouns with many prior adjectives, or over-many adjectival or adverbial phrases? Does he use words which are metaphorical, or indulge in more unusual figures of speech or use irony or use words in a sense different from that to which the child is used (e.g. he was a *brilliant* student, *secretary* of state, public *servant*)?
- When the author uses pronouns like 'he' and 'they', is it always clear what these refer to?
- Can you detect anything that is ambiguous (e.g. the famous Chomsky example, 'Visiting relatives can be a nuisance.')?
- Is the text legible and the layout clear? Here the teacher will want to look at such matters as the size of print and whether or not the lines of text are justified, which can sometimes cause awkward word splits. (Justified text is where the right-hand margin is regulated in the same way as the left-hand margin usually is.) Are headings and sub-headings clear? Are illustrations close to the text referring to them?

Readability measures applied to worksheets

The application of readability measures to worksheets presents problems, as this passage shows:

Readability measures are statistical tools, and it is up to

the teacher to decide whether it is appropriate to apply them to a text. Generally speaking, it is only valid to use a formula on narrative or expository prose, and any deviation from this can be dangerous. Worksheets present an obvious problem: many worksheets are a mixture of headings, brief instructions and more continuous prose, and yet many teachers would want to evaluate them using a formula. This can only be done if (a) the analysis is confined to continuous prose, and (b) there is an absolute minimum of 50 words for analysis, and preferably 100 or more. (*Readability in the Classroom* by Colin Harrison, CUP, 1980)

The kinds of teacher judgement discussed in the previous section are, perhaps, more relevant to most worksheets. And, of course, difficulties concerning language level will reveal themselves in the first 'run' of any new material and in the type of difficulty emerging through your diagnostic tests. Chapter 8 considers ways of evaluating worksheets; but one point worth making here, and already mentioned in Chapter 1, is that construction of worksheets should not be a lone activity. You are more likely to eliminate unsuitable language if other teachers read your worksheets. As I have mentioned earlier in this chapter, pooled teachers' judgements are more reliable than individual judgements.

A checklist

- Are your worksheets presented within the context of oral explanation? Are new words highlighted and explained?
- Are the information and instructions in your worksheets written in a way that is completely understood by your pupils?
- Are textbooks, extracts and other written source material, which are used in conjunction with your worksheets, presented at a language level appropriate to the age and ability of your pupils?
- Do the activities generated by your worksheets maintain a balance between writing, talking, listening and reading?
- In demanding extended writing from your pupils, do you help them through the earlier stages of formulating ideas, making notes, drafting and redrafting, before they produce a final copy?
- Whatever your subject, do your worksheets reflect a responsibility for the language development of your pupils?

Further reading list

Reading ability and language development are so central to all learning and have so many aspects allied to the main theme of this book, that this chapter could have expanded into a book of its own. Unlike the other chapters, therefore, this one has a reading list.

Barnes, D., Britton, J. & Rosen, H., *Language, The Learner and the School*, Penguin

BBC Adult Literacy Handbook, BBC, 1975

Binns, R., *From Speech to Writing*, Scottish Curriculum Development Service, 1978

Gatherer, W.A. & Jeffs, R.B., *Language Through the Secondary Curriculum*, Holmes McDougall, 1980

Harrison, C., *Readability in the Classroom*, CUP, 1980

A Language for Life (The Bullock Report), HMSO, 1975

Humphrey, P.D., *Reading: Test and Assessment Techniques*, Hodder & Stoughton, 1976

Marland, M., et al, *Language across the Curriculum*, Heinemann, 1977

Stibbs, A., *Assessing Children's Language*, National Association for the Teaching of English

Walker, C., *Reading Development and Extension*, Ward Lock, 1974

Chapter Seven

Worksheets for less able pupils

The ease with which a pupil grasps the point of what you have written is not simply a matter of the reading age of the material. We have considered the application of readability formulae to existing texts in the previous chapter, but experience has shown that attempts to write worksheets according to these formulae may sometimes result in prose which produces low reading-age scores, not prose which poor readers can understand.

Whether or not a worksheet proves too difficult depends also on the degree of abstraction, the difficulty of the underlying concept, the amount of information on the page and the way it is presented visually, the relevance of the material to the pupil and his general level of motivation. Perhaps the most important factors are how the point being taught in the worksheet is integrated with the course as a whole, what the supporting framework of introduction and explanation has been, whether the pupil is ready for that particular concept, and whether it has been introduced in the correct learning sequence.

Some general points

- Build on your pupils' existing knowledge – it is preferable to build up a concept, starting from what they know, rather than to use a term and follow it up with examples. For instance, for the concept of 'authority' start with parents, teachers, bosses in Saturday jobs; for the concept of 'society', start with the family, the peergroup, the class.
- Assignments should relate to a pupil's personal experience, e.g. 'Describe any pollution *you* see on your way to school.'
- Tasks should be self-contained and all information needed readily accessible.
- Repeat tasks in various forms for reinforcement. Once is not enough. Slow learners are apt to forget fast.
- Learning sequences should be broken down into small steps.
- Keep the filling in of blanks to a minimum. Pupils learn more if they have to write out complete sentences.
- Slow learners need success and at as high a level as possible.

Making your meaning clear

Keep sentences short and use familiar words. Specialist terminology should not be omitted, but it is important that such words should be spoken out loud and displayed on the blackboard *before* pupils are asked to write them. Where unfamiliar words have to be introduced these must be drawn to the pupils' attention – e.g. explained in an introductory lesson (orally or on an OHP); underlined in the text (which might indicate they should be looked up in a dictionary); the meaning explained in brackets after the words; key words placed in contexts that lead up to them and help clarify their meaning; a 'word-bank' supplied on the same page. New words should be heard, seen, spelled, written, used and re-used. Sometimes it helps to hyphenate words to make their meaning, pronunciation or recognition clearer.

Avoid using words ambiguously – e.g. 'Man *acts* on his environment'; 'The German planes dived out of the sun' (does this mean their opponents had the sun in their eyes, or does it mean that the planes went behind clouds?). Be careful about words which have both a common and a specialist meaning:

> *volume* – many pupils in the first year of secondary school associate this with the knob on their TV set rather than with measurement;
> *suspension* – what comes to mind first is not particles suspended in liquid, but what happens to a footballer if he misbehaves;
> *state* – not a political unit, but the condition your mother was in last night;
> *revolution* – has different meanings in Geography, Physics, English and History;
> *solution* – has a different meaning in Mathematics than it has in Chemistry.

Other words can easily acquire strange, but logical, meanings – e.g. coalfield (a field with lumps of coal scattered over it); watershed (a kind of houseboat).

Remember, too, that abbreviations may need explanation – e.g. approx., i.e., NATO, EEC.

Writing questions, tasks and assignments

Teachers sometimes lapse into a more difficult vocabulary when it comes to writing questions – e.g. 'identify' instead of 'name'; 'Opposite each phrase write the *corresponding* piece of information.'; '*Outline* the main points.' Try to use ordinary words.

Allow enough space on your worksheet for the pupil to answer. Less able pupils often have large, ungainly writing. But remember that pupils tend to associate the number of dashes or dots in a blank space with the number of letters or words required for the answer.

Make instructions, questions and assignments stand out from the main text. They can be in upper case, in different type or boxed off. Never give more than one instruction per line - place instructions like a list, one beneath the other.

Make sure your instructions come *before* the reading required - e.g. 'Copy and label the diagram below', *not* 'Copy and label the diagram above.'

It is easier to follow an instruction if the sequence complies with the temporal order. Compare these two sentences:

The powder must be placed in the machine and the lid closed before it is switched on.
Before the machine is switched on, the lid must be closed and the powder placed in it.

Remedial pupils need a great deal of direction. Questions for assignments, tasks, worksheets etc. must be framed in a way that leads pupils to the answer. Questions must be absolutely straightforward - no variety of interpretation, or answers depending upon variable factors, no double-barrelled questions. Ask what *they* think, then at least you will get an answer. For example, instead of 'Why do you think the family in the story did not want to move?', a better question would be 'Why would *you* not want to move?'

If the pupil is referred to a book for independent reading, have you thoroughly vetted the relevant section as to its readability?

Structuring your sentences

An important factor in making what you write easily understood is sentence stucture.

Avoid complex and compound sentences with more than one idea or fact in them:

They heavily outnumbered the invaders, yet in the end the Spaniards won because they were brave, because they had better weapons, because many Indians took their side and because many Aztecs suffered from a terrible disease called smallpox which came from Europe with the invaders.

Remember, however, that ease of comprehension is not directly related to shortness of sentence. Compression can also cause difficulty.

Avoid qualifying phrases:

Whether the difference is great or small and whether true north lies east or west of Magnetic North depends on the position of the observer at the Earth's surface.

Avoid qualifying words such as 'probably', 'fairly', 'to some extent'.

Sentences with subordinate clauses, particularly if they come *before* the main part of the sentence, are difficult for less able pupils to understand.

Stick to one simple definition, rather than giving alternatives as in 'The electric current or the rate at which the electrons are flowing must be the same all round the circuit.'

Avoid negatives, especially double negatives as in 'The figures provide no indication that costs would not have been lower if competition had not been restricted.'

Sentences are easier to understand when written in the active voice rather than the passive voice. For example, 'The staff will hold a meeting next week' is better than 'A meeting will be held by the staff next week.'

Layout, type and illustrations

Large areas of unrelieved print can be boring - use short passages only, broken up by pictures. Page layout is very important in aiding learning for less able pupils. Try not to have more than one teaching/learning point per page. Example 11 illustrates these points.

There should be consistency in layout, in numbering, use of symbols etc., and continuity in graphics. Each new step should contain something recognizable from the previous step.

Reading matter should be typed - pupils learn to read from the printed page - handwritten work only adds to their difficulties. Some remedial experts advise the use of capital letters, others say that these should only be used in simple sentence instructions. In longer passages it is confusing because capitals are normally a signal for the start of a new sentence or a place name.

Make sure words are adequately spaced and lines are not too long. Ten words per line is best.

The size of the printing is important. Poor readers need larger print than do good readers, and less reading to a page. When pupils are asked to write a response the print should be of a similar size to the letters that they commonly use so that the page looks uniform when finished. Different sizes of print can be used to make an item stand out or to show its relative importance.

Sub-headings should be reduced to a minimum as too many are confusing. Similarly, heavy type or underlined words should be limited to key words throughout the text.

Diagrams should be simple and uncluttered, and if possible enlarged to A4 size for clarity. Tracing and shading exercises help with spatial understanding.

Illustrations should be accompanied by text. Remember that pictures containing human activity are more interesting. Where possible, reinforce sketches with good quality photographs. Also, use comic strip and diagrams where apt.

Maps

Maps should be large enough to work with and write on. However, throughout your unit stick to the same projection and scale and keep the same alignment throughout (e.g. North at the top of the page).

Less able pupils often find it difficult to tell which is the land and which is the sea. If the sea is shaded, much confusion is avoided.

Be consistent in whether you write the name of a town to the right, left, top or bottom of the appropriate dot or shaded area.

Place maps in their context. The outlines of some countries can be difficult to recognize if reproduced on their own. Also, place a box around a map to show where it begins and ends.

Further thoughts

You can probably add many useful suggestions of your own to those in this chapter. Remedial experts vary in their approaches and have different opinions as to which are the most effective methods.

Probably above all, provide variety of activity. Provide plenty of non-reading/writing activities – e.g. drawing, colouring, tracing, games, puzzles, simulations, crosswords, word-search. For the sake of variety, workcards might sometimes be used in place of worksheets (they also tend to be shorter and less daunting).

Although some suggestions have been given here about clear and simple writing, the most effective approach to a teaching point may not be to present it in written form. Always bear the alternatives in mind (see Figure 39, overleaf).

Case study 12
This study is of an exercise for a mixed-ability class of 14-year-old children, at Albert Secondary School, Glasgow.

Mainstream version

BEING INSIDE

Prison cells are mostly small and colourless. Originally designed for one person, each cell measures 4 metres × 2½ metres and is 3 metres high. There is a high barred window for ventilation and light and the cell door has a Judas hole.

The furniture consists of: iron bed, wooden table, chair, washstand with jug, basin and chamber pot.

Prisoners are issued with a blanket, 2 sheets, a mattress, a night shirt, a towel, a spoon and a mug. The money which a prisoner earns is usually spent on articles such as tobacco, chocolate, writing paper and pens.

Prisoners have a language of their own, e.g.:

'Screws' – prison officers
'Bird cage' – prison
'Snout' – tobacco
'Sleep' – 6 months to 1 year sentence
'Stretch' – sentence over 4 years

Remedial version

BEING INSIDE

Prison cells are small and dull. They were built to hold one person. They are 4 metres long, 2½ metres broad and 3 metres high. Up high is a window with bars. This is for air (ventilation) and light. The cell door has a Judas hole.

The furniture is – an iron bed
a wooden table
a chair
a washstand with jug
a basin and a chamber pot

Prisoners get a blanket, 2 sheets, a nightshirt, a towel, a mattress, a spoon and a mug. On the wall there is a list of the prison rules.

Prison work is a privilege (something good).

If a prisoner does not behave, this privilege can be taken away from him. The prisoner gets a wage. He spends it on tobacco, sweets, writing paper and pens. Prisoners have their own language:

SCREWS – prison officers
BIRD CAGE – prison
SNOUT – tobacco
SLEEP – 6 months to 1 year
STRETCH – over 4 years

Comment
Notice the following differences between the remedial and mainstream versions:

- The sentences are shorter and simpler.
- Instead of describing the cell as '4 metres × 2½ metres' it is described as '4 metres long, 2½ metres broad'.
- The word 'ventilation' is explained.
- 'The furniture consists of' is changed to 'The furniture is' and the items listed are rearranged to one per line.
- Words are underlined for further explanation by the teacher.
- The mainstream version does not explain how it is that prisoners get wages. In the remedial version this is explained.
- The words of the 'special language' are taken out of inverted commas and instead put into upper case.

Example 11

MALNUTRITION

One out of ten people in the world does not get enough to eat.

Six out of ten do not get the RIGHT KIND OF FOOD. When people do not get a balanced diet they suffer from MALNUTRITION. This leads to illness and often death.

Things to do

Look at the world map showing hunger and poverty. Using your atlas and the map – write down 10 countries with MALNUTRITION problems.

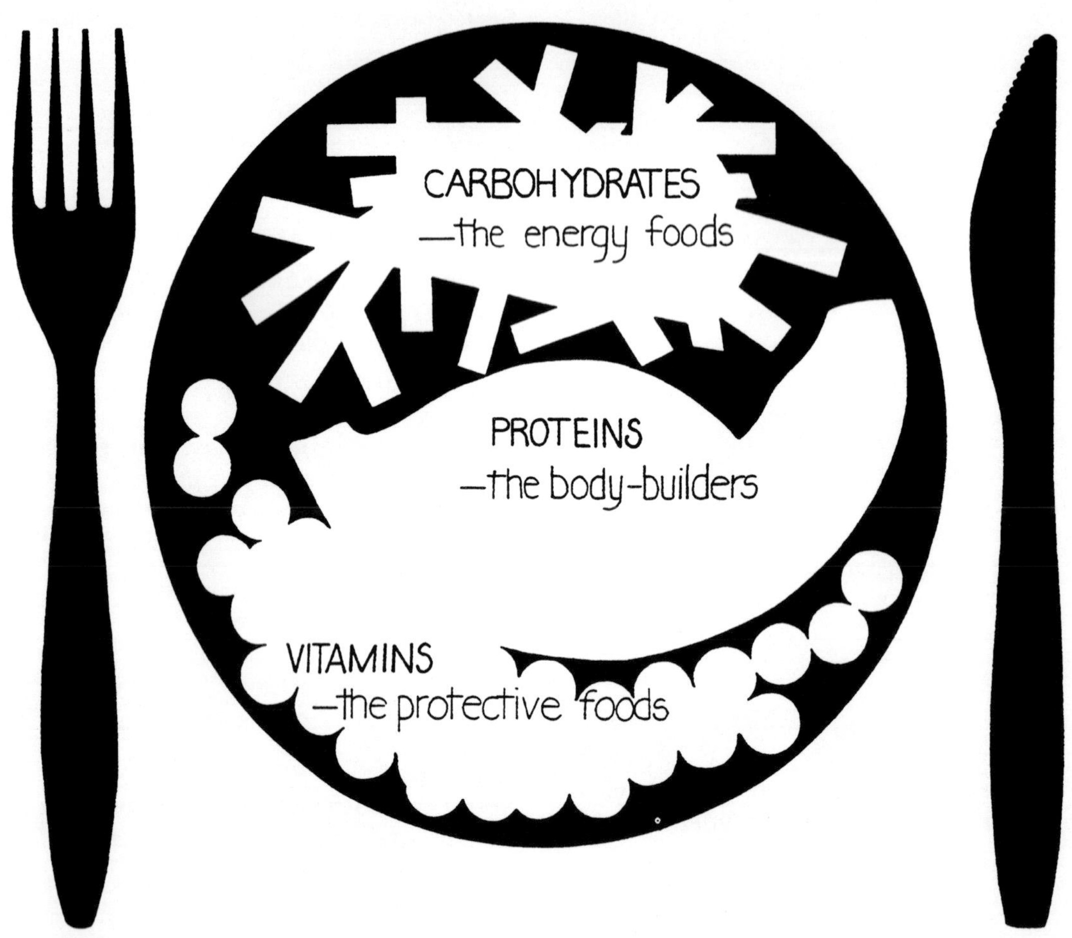

We need three things in our food.

Things to do

Use the diagram above to help you write in the meanings of these three words:

CARBOHYDRATES ....

PROTEINS ....

VITAMINS ....

Figure 39 *Example 11*

Mainstream (or core) version

WHERE AM I ?

Fill in the table below:

PLACE : ROOM ____.____, G __________ D __________ ,

G __________ H ____ S ____ .

TOWN : ____________________

REGION : ____________________

COUNTRY : ____________________

CONTINENT : ____________________

The 'address' above describes, in words, your exact location or POSITION and would allow, for example, a letter posted 12 000 miles away in Australia to reach you easily.

In Geography, the word POSITION is an important word. We must be able to state the position of features such as cities, mountains, lakes, etc. on the Earth's surface.

One simple way of telling a position is to use distance and direction. THE COMPASS allows us to give DIRECTION.

Name all the points shown on the diagram below.

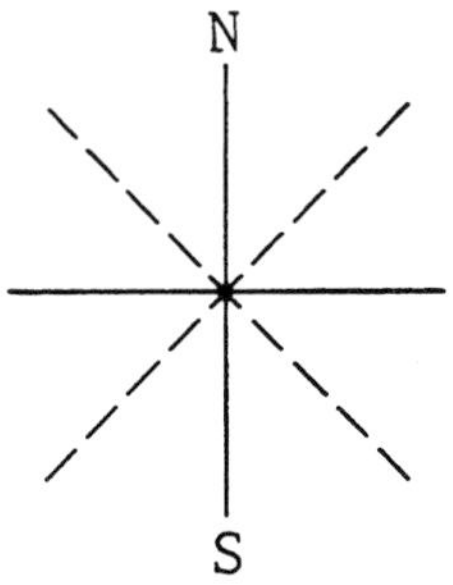

N

S

Using this compass we can give the direction from one place to another.

Example:

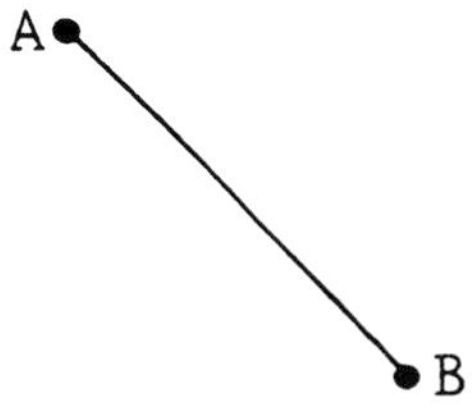

A

B

What is the position of Town A from Town B?

Answer: North West

Complete the following exercises:

1. X Y

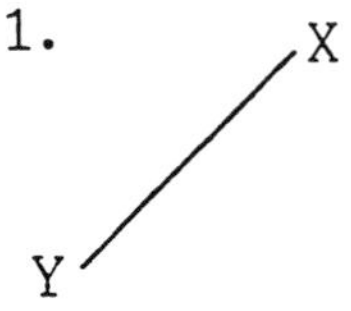

What is the position of Town X from Town Y?

Answer: __________

2. Q P

What is the position of Town P from Q?

Answer: __________

3. W Y X

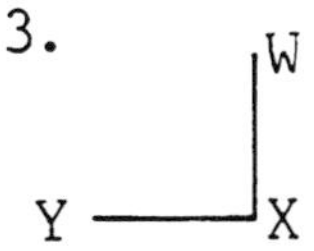

Leaving point W, what directions would you follow to pass through X and Y ?

Answer: ________________

4. A B C D

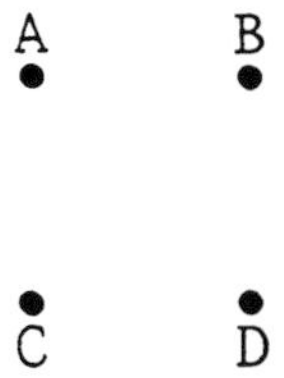

On the diagram, join up the points in the following order - A,B,C,D,A- now state the direction followed between each point.

Answer: A - B __________, B - C __________,

C - D __________, D - A __________.

Figure 40 *Case study 13*

Revision exercise

THE COMPASS

FILL IN ALL THE POINTS OF THE COMPASS ON THE DIAGRAM DRAWN FOR YOU BELOW.

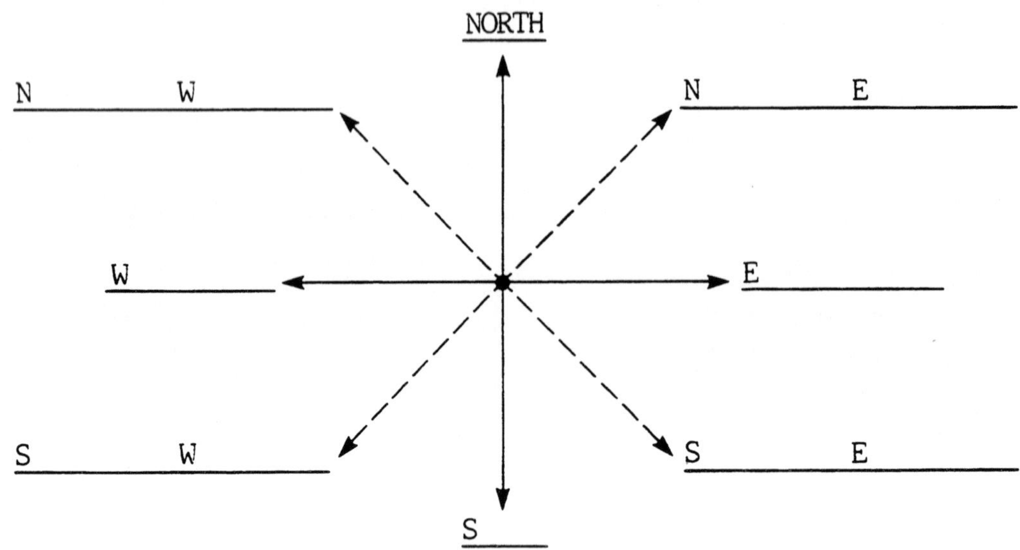

2. DRAW THE DIAGRAM IN YOUR JOTTER AGAIN. THIS TIME USE LETTERS FOR THE DIRECTION AND NOT THE FULL WORD.

EXAMPLE: SOUTH EAST becomes S.E.

3. YOU CAN USE THE POINTS OF THE COMPASS TO TELL SOMEONE WHICH DIRECTION TO GO IN FROM ONE PLACE TO ANOTHER.

EXAMPLE TO FIND OUT THE DIRECTION FROM POINT 0 TO TOWN A.

i. FILL IN THE POINTS OF THE COMPASS DRAWN BESIDE POINT 0.

ii. WHICH DIRECTION WOULD YOU FOLLOW TO GO TO TOWN A?

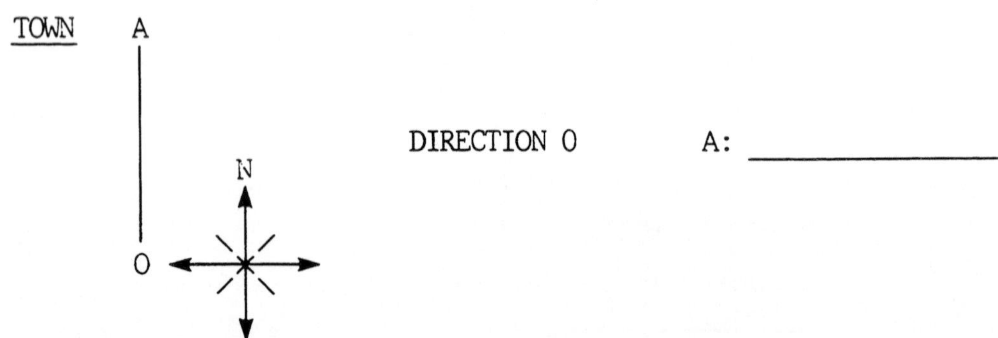

EXERCISE: TRY ALL THE EXAMPLES ON THE NEXT PAGE. DRAW A SMALL COMPASS BESIDE POINT 0 FIRST OF ALL.

Figure 41 *Case study 13*

Direction exercise (2)

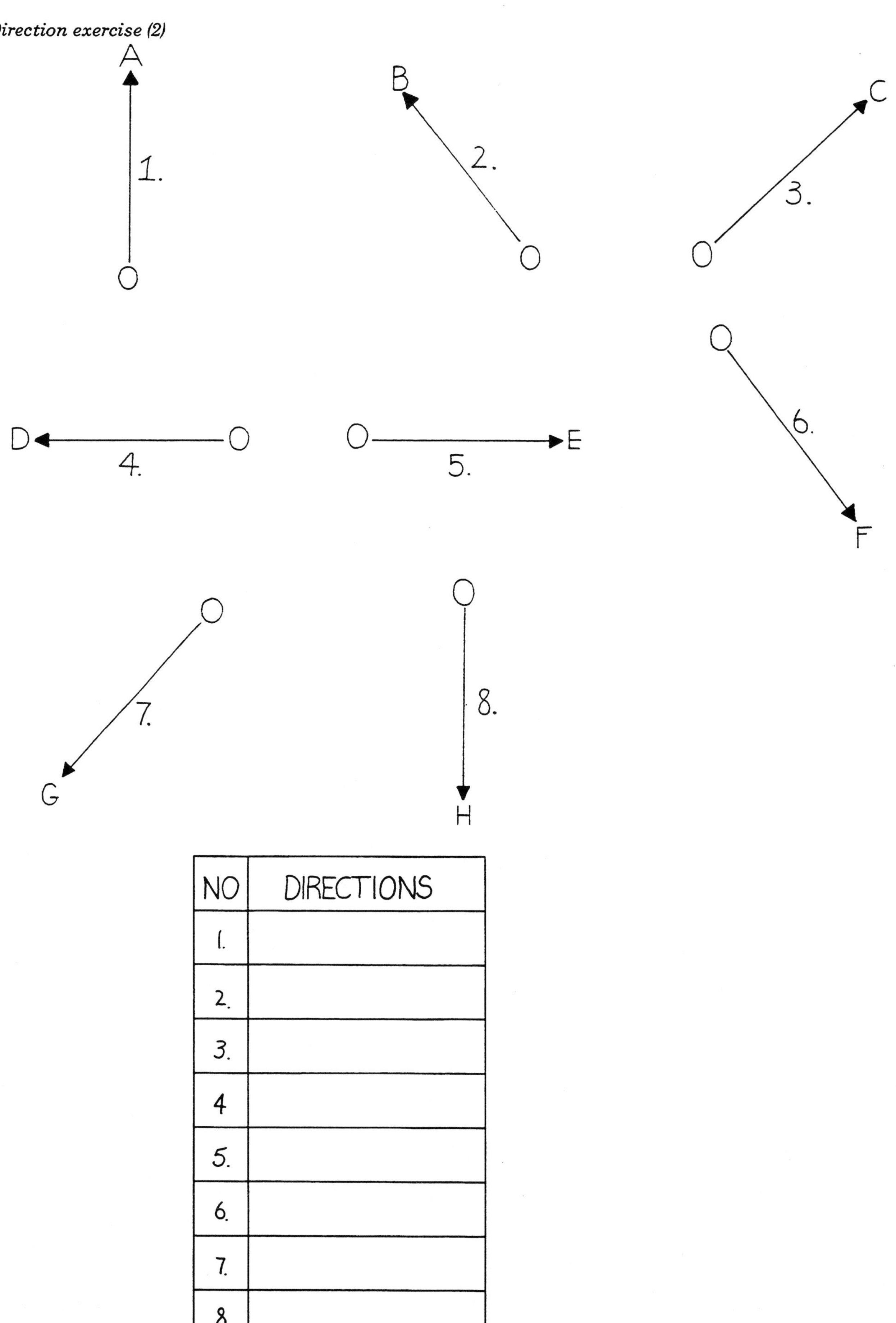

NO	DIRECTIONS
1.	
2.	
3.	
4	
5.	
6.	
7.	
8.	

Figure 42 *Case study 13*

Source: Geography Dept., Greenfaulds High School, Cumbernauld.

Case study 13
The sheets, Figs. 40–42, pp. 65–67, were used with a mixed-ability group of 12-year-olds.

Comment
Some of the main points to note here are:

- In the revision (remedial) version the lettering is bigger, it is more spaced out and there is less information on the page.
- Smaller learning steps are used. For example, finding the direction from one point to another is done in two steps in the mainstream version and in three steps in the remedial version.
- More cues or clues are used in the remedial version, e.g. giving the first letter on the points of the compass (N______ W______).
- Reinforcement is given in the remedial version, e.g. 'Draw the diagram in your jotter again. This time use letters for the direction and not the full word.'
- In the remedial version, examples are given at each step by way of explanation.

Chapter Eight

A stormy passage

In this chapter I take one case study and use it to illustrate some of the points made in the preceding chapters. Although the prose passage under consideration is about the Spanish Armada, the discussion surrounding it should be relevant to all subjects.

First, alternative methods of conveying the information are discussed (this is based on an example from *How to write a Distance Learning Course*, Council for Educational Technology, 1980). The readability level is then calculated using a number of different formulae.

This is followed by a look at possible ways in which a worksheet on this topic could generate expressive writing and an awareness of different types of audience.

Finally, looking forward to Chapter 9, the visual quality of the page is studied and an alternative layout is presented.

Case study 14

The Armada: version A
About 1585 Philip II seems to have decided to make a great attack on England. Unlike Elizabeth, he possessed an army large enough to conquer a country. Even so he had to build or rather to increase his fleet; the Mediterranean galleys which won the battle of Lepanto against the Turks were of little use in the stormy waters of the Channel or the wide Atlantic. Philip's plan, as finally settled, was to land the Spanish army of the Netherlands in England under cover of a protecting fleet which would also carry a large force from Spain. He expected, in view of reports from catholic exiles, that the English catholics would welcome him. In fact, most catholics would have fought against him as stoutly on land as they had fought at sea, but it is doubtful whether a united English resistance would have been strong enough to meet the best-trained army under the Duke of Parma, the first soldier of the age.

Fortunately for England, the test was not applied. In April 1587, Drake sailed into Cadiz harbour to destroy many thousand tons of shipping and stores. Until the end of June, Drake's ships harassed all traffic along the coasts of the peninsula. Hence the Armada was not ready before the winter. The last preparations were not completed until May 1588, and the Spanish ships were not sighted off the Lizard until 19 July. The Armada was an imposing sight, but half of it was made up of heavily laden transport and supply ships. In fighting strength they were superior because their ships were faster, more easily handled, and built primarily as gun-carriers, whereas the Spanish ships, though heavily armed, still had the high superstructures designed for the old type of boarding warfare. The English divided their forces: a western fleet - the larger of the two - was to prevent a direct landing, while an eastern fleet kept Parma from sending out his transports. The western fleets followed the Armada up the Channel, 'plucking their feathers', yet failing to break their unity. The weakest point of Philip's plan, however, was the junction between the great fleet and Parma's transports. The transports could not come out unless they were protected from English attack; the nearest port deep enough to take the Armada was Flushing, and Flushing was in English and Dutch hands.

In the afternoon of 27 July, the Armada anchored off Calais. About midnight on 28/29 July the English, now joined by the eastern fleet, sent eight fireships against the Spaniards and drove them out in confusion. Next day, in a running fight along the coast towards Dunkirk, the range and weight of the English guns decided the issue. The Spanish Admiral could not turn back through the Channel; he was compelled to take the long course home round the British Isles. He had no pilots for these northern and western waters; the winds, which had favoured the Spanish plans in July, now completed their ruin. Late in September the remnants of the Spanish fleet entered Santander. Sixty-three Spanish ships - very nearly half the Armada - had been lost. On the English side not one ship was sunk or captured.

The Armada: version B
This is given in full in Figure 43, p. 70.

The Armada: version C
This is given in full in Figure 44, p. 71.

Assessment of case study 14

From the *teaching* point of view, you might consider whether you want to emphasize facts or opinions. The cartoon suggests that Drake was a hero and Philip of Spain a silly. Cartoons are an excellent way of presenting opinions; lists on the other hand are not.

Figure 43 *Case study 14 - version B*

THE COURSE OF THE ARMADA		
1587	April	Drake destroys stores and boats in Cadiz harbour.
	May/June	Drake patrols Spanish coast, harassing ships.
	Summer/ Autumn	Spain prepares Armada
	Winter	Ships ready
1588	Spring	Final preparations
	July 19	Armada sighted off England
	July 20-28	Tries to link with forces in Netherlands so army can be protected while crossing channel. English ships keep forces apart.
	July 28	English send fireships into Spanish fleet off Calais. Spanish flee and are compelled to make the tour round Britain.
	End Sept.	Remnants of fleet arrive back in Spain. 63 ships lost.

Figure 44 *Case study 14 - version C*

It is well worth reminding ourselves of the varied roles that illustrations can serve, e.g.

- they arouse interest;
- they can communicate certain kinds of information more effectively than words;
- they can condense complex material.

From the *writing* point of view, when we start to write we often simply put pen to paper and let (or attempt to let) the sentences flow. We simply forget other possible styles of presentation.

Perhaps, then, we should consider combining visual and verbal presentation. If we present the same idea or argument in two different forms we are increasing the chances that students will make those connections and grasp the whole. At the same time we will reinforce our teaching so that points are more likely to be remembered.

Version C is a fairly simple example of information mapping as an alternative to a straight prose passage. Figures 45 and 46 (pp. 72 and 73) elaborate further on this.

Readability

The first paragraph of the prose passage of version A was analysed by 'Textgrader' (Hutchinson Computer Software), with the following results:

Formula	*Readability level*
Mugford	13.74
Smog	16.83
Forecast	15.43
Fry	15.25
Flesch	15.25

Textgrader gave the coordinates for the Fry Graph as $x = 4.42$ and $y = 152.21$ which, when plotted on the graph (see Chapter 6, Figure 35) gave a readability level of 15.25.

Towards the end of Chapter 6, under the heading 'Teachers' judgements', various criteria were mentioned which, in general, seem to be the basis for such judgements about texts. Applying these criteria to the Armada text, a teacher reported:

Although events are in chronological order, various issues are introduced which divert the reader from the main story - e.g. the attitude of the English catholics, aspects of naval architecture. A broad canvas is compressed into a fairly short space, almost every sentence containing several learning points or ideas. A less able pupil would assimilate only a fraction of these facts.

Without a map, it is difficult to build up a mental image of what is happening and to visualize where the various places mentioned in the passage are in relation to each other.

The passage assumes familiarity with a fairly wide range of historical knowledge to do with the period. For some pupils this would be a false assumption and would impair a full understanding of the passage. The structure of the sentences is very complex, being full of subordinate clauses and qualifying phrases. For example, in the sentence (continued on p. 74).

INFORMATION MAPPING

Introduction	Information mapping means using a page like a map or a chart so that, through the physical layout and format, the learner can find his way from one point to another. Information mapping also assumes that the content is selected and organised according to a set of underlying principles. The methods of presentation are the visible features. The organisation of content is the invisible feature.
Visible Features	• Information presented in blocks, with a marginal label for each block. • Consistant format for each kind of information. Different formats for different kinds of information. • Uniform headings and subheadings for easy scanning and reference. • Questions and answers located close to information map and always in the same position on the page.
Invisible Features	The sequence and arrangement of material presented in information maps is a result of • Specification of learning objectives. • Classification of the skills and learning experiences involved. • Analysis of the learning steps required.

Figure 45 *Visible and invisible features of information map books* (*source: Designing Instructional Text* by James Hartley, 1978)

If cost is limited, travel by Rocket. However, if time is also limited, travel by Super-Rocket. If cost is the only limiting factor, a Stellacar is best for journeys of less than 12 orbs. For longer journeys a Satellite should be used. When there are no limits on time or cost, a Gallactibus is best - except when journeys exceed 12 orbs, in which case, go by Starship.

Limit on cost only

Go by Rocket

Limit on time only

Go by Satellite for journeys of more than 12 orbs,
Go by Stellacar for journeys of less than 12 orbs.

Limit on both time and cost

Go by Super-Rocket.

No limit on both time and cost

Go by Starship for journeys of more than 12 orbs,
Go by Gallactibus for journeys of less than 12 orbs.

	Journey less than 12 orbs	Journey more than 12 orbs
Limit on cost only	Go by Rocket	Go by Rocket
Limit on time only	Go by Stellacar	Go by Satellite
Limit on both cost and time	Go by Super-Rocket	Go by Super-Rocket
No Limit on time or cost	Go by Gallactibus	Go by Starship

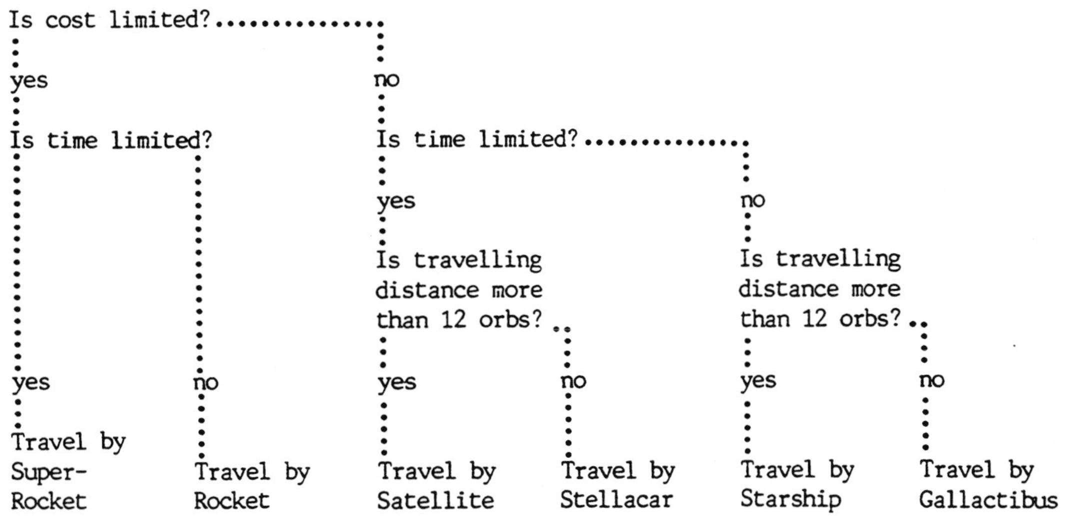

Figure 46 *Another example of information mapping*

'*Philip's plan*, as finally settled, *was to land the Spanish army* of the Netherlands *in England* under cover of a protective fleet which would also carry a large force from Spain.

the main piece of information (in italics) is so surrounded by 'extras' that it might be hidden from any but a well practised eye.

There are many words and phrases which would cause difficulty or confusion to a poor reader of limited vocabulary. For example

the first soldier of the age
in view of reports
harassed all traffic
superstructure
boarding warfare
the weight of guns

There is an ambiguity in the middle part of the passage:

'The Armada was an imposing sight, but half of it was made up of heavily laden transports and supply ships. In fighting strength *they* were superior because. . .'

The word 'they' refers to the English ships, though this is far from obvious in the text.

Visually, the text is daunting, being almost a whole page of unbroken print, single-spaced and in fairly small print.

Used at an instructional level and with a great deal of support and explanation, it might just be suitable for 14-year-olds; but more suitable for 15+. Probably, it would be better to use this in conjunction with a simplified version for the slower learner.

One simplified version, constructed by a Remedial Specialist, reads like this:

In 1588 Philip II decided to attack England. Philip had many soldiers. He had to build more ships to carry all his soldiers to England. He had one army in the Netherlands and one army in Spain. Philip's plan was to bring both armies to England.

The Spanish army was the best in the world. The English army might have been defeated.

The readability levels of this passage, when analysed by the different formula, are compared below with those given for the original passage:

Formula	*Remedial version*	*Original version*
Mugford	8.50	13.74
Smog	11.87	16.83
Forecast	13.1	15.43
Fry	8.6	15.25
Flesch	11.34	15.25

Expressive writing

In Chapter 4 we saw how both pupil talk and expressive writing were essential to 'internalizing' knowledge. Table 11 suggests the kind of outlets for expressive writing which a passage like 'The Armada' could generate. In order to present this in tabular form, some of the activities have not been detailed in full. Some pupils, for example, would need more help than the instructions given – e.g. guidelines in the form of suggested headings; topics which should be mentioned; key words or phrases which should be used; more pictures to look at; group activity rather than an individual task.

Some possibilities for how the pupil can write for an audience other than the teacher are also suggested. Other possibilities, not mentioned in Table 11, open up with such arrangements as twinning of classes, exchange of letters between different schools, individual 'pen-pal' arrangements, a combined History and English project.

All of the ideas in Table 11 could be effected through the medium of worksheets. Of course, they are not all aimed at the same level of ability. Some would obviously be more suited to extension work.

Visual presentation

The teacher's report on the Armada text commented on the lack of a map and on the daunting unbroken mass of words. As an exercise in layout, without attempting to alter the text, version D shows how a little thought to layout and design can vastly improve the visual impact, increase motivation to read it and generate more positive attitudes towards it (see Figure 47, pp. 76–7). Note in particular:

- The prose is more spaced out, taking two pages instead of one.
- The pages are framed to keep the eye inside the main area.
- There is a title or heading and this area is kept simple and spacious.
- The typeface chosen for the heading is in keeping with the subject and not a modern typeface.
- On the first page the ship is sailing from right to left and on the second page it is sailing from left to right – in both cases it is leading the eye back into the text. (Remember this when drawing strip cartoons – the first picture should have something leading the eye to the right and the end picture on the line should direct you back to the start of the next line.)
- Both ships have plenty of space around them and both serve to break the text into half-page columns, breaking up the mass of print.

Table 11

Writing about the Armada

Type of activity in worksheet	*Awareness of audience*	*Comment*
Imagine you are a commander on one of Drake's ships. Either write an entry in your diary for a day in late July 1588, or write a letter to your family describing the events of that month as you saw them.	Different kind of writing for self (diary) or for family (letter).	One problem about this is that someone who *was* actually there would probably produce an account which would make a teacher despair - preoccupied with trivia, unaware of the overview of the battle, full of self flattery etc.
Write a poem or the lyrics for a song about anything to do with the Spanish Armada which excited or interested you.	Possibly the rest of the class (peer group)	Work could be displayed on the wall.
Write a description of the sea battle intended to help an artist paint a picture of the event.	Public/adult other than teacher	This could be done in pairs, with each translating the other's description into graphic form. Opportunities for task orientated talk here.
Prepare notes for a short lecture to the rest of the class about - (some specific aspect) e.g. design of galleys, firearms in the late 16th Century, a short biography of Phillip II.	Notes for self, lecture for peer group.	Pupil should be encouraged to create and use visual aids to accompany the mini-lecture. Questions from the audience could generate useful talk.
Write a short play based on the story of Drake at Plymouth Ho.	There could be a tangible audience for this.	If done as a group activity, much learning through talk might take place. Possibilities here for use of tape recorder or video camera.
Write a brief account of the Armada, telling it from the point of view of the Captain of a Spanish galleon who has returned home to his friends.	Public/adult other than teacher.	This could be read out to class (more audience) and compared with the English point of view in activity 1.
Write an account for your parents about what you are doing in history, what are the most important things you have learned about the Armada and what interested you most.	Parents	If you have some kind of pupil folio into which they put their best work for taking home to parents, display on open days etc., this also creates a sense of audience. The exercise of evaluating and selecting work for the folio is a valuable learning experience for the pupil.

King Philip II

THE SPANISH ARMADA

Queen Elizabeth I

Fortunately for England, the test was not applied. In April 1587 Drake sailed into Cadiz harbour to destroy many thousand tons of shipping and stores. Until the end of June, Drake's ships harassed all traffic along the coasts of the peninsula. Hence the Armada was not ready before the winter. The last preparations were not completed until May 1588, and the Spanish ships were not sighted off the Lizard until July 19. The Armada was an imposing sight, but half of it was made up of heavily laden transports and supply ships. In fighting ships of war the English were almost as strong. In fighting strength they were superior because their ships were faster, more easily handled, and built primarily as gun-carriers whereas the Spanish ships, though heavily armed, still had the high superstructures designed for the old type of boarding warfare. The English divided their forces: a western fleet - the larger of the two - was to prevent a direct landing, while an eastern fleet kept Parma from sending out his transports. The western fleets followed the Armada up the Channel, 'plucking their feathers', yet failing to break their unity. The weakest point of Philip's plan, however, was the junction between the great fleet and Parma's transports. The transports could not come out unless they were protected from English attack; the nearest port deep enough to take the Armada was Flushing, and Flushing was in English and Dutch hands.

About 1585 Philip II seems to have decided to make a great attack on England. Unlike Elizabeth, he possessed an army large enough to conquer a country. Even so he had to build or rather to increase his fleet; the Mediterranean galleys which won the battle of Lepanto against the Turks were of little use in the stormy waters of the Channel or the wide Atlantic. Philip's plan, as finally settled, was to land the Spanish army of the Netherlands in England under cover of a protecting fleet which would also carry a large force from Spain. He expected, in view of reports from catholic exiles, that the English catholics would welcome him. In fact, most catholics would have fought against him as stoutly on land as they fought at sea, but it is doubtful whether a united English resistance would have been strong enough to meet the best-trained army under the Duke of Parma, the first soldier of the age.

Figure 47 *Case study 14 - version D*

Jesus of Lubek, sunk at San Juan in 1568

Drake's flag-ship, the *Revenge*

MAP SHOWING PROGRESS OF ACTION

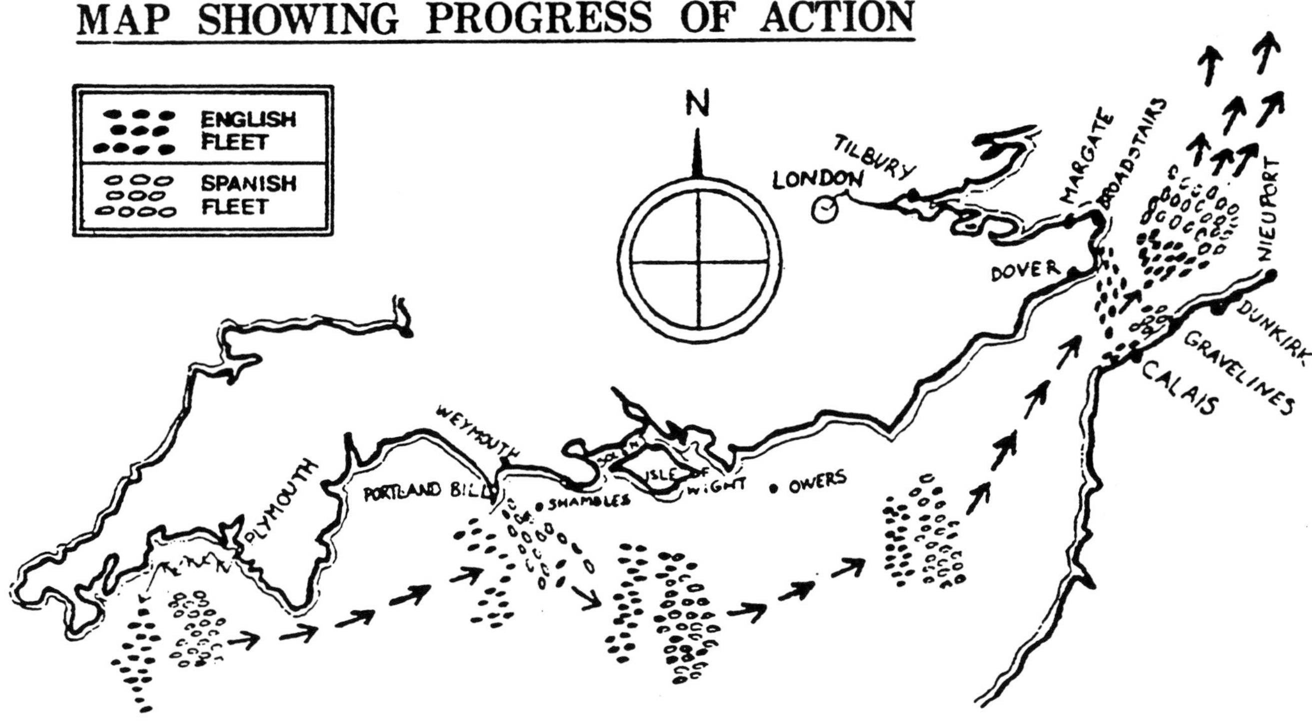

In the afternoon of July 27 the Armada anchored off Calais. About midnight on July 28-9 the English, now joined by the eastern fleet, sent eight fireships against the Spaniards and drove them out in confusion. Next day, in a running fight along the coast towards Dunkirk, the range and weight of the English guns decided the issue. The Spanish Admiral could not turn back through the Channel; he was compelled to take the long course home round the British Isles. He had no pilots for these northern and western waters; the winds, which had favoured the Spanish plans in July, now completed their ruin. Late in September the remnants of the Spanish fleet entered Santander. Sixty-three Spanish ships - very nearly half the Armada - had been lost. On the English side not one ship was sunk or captured.

Chapter Nine

The eyes have it

Textbooks have certain drawbacks in that they cannot closely reflect the interests and ability levels of your pupils; and marketing considerations make it difficult to pitch a book entirely at one particular teaching strategy, mode of assessment or syllabus. However, textbooks do have the great advantage of being professionally printed, with professionally produced graphics and facilities for colour plates etc. On the other hand, teacher-produced material, while being geared to the specific needs of particular children and reflecting current educational thinking, is often amateur in its production and sometimes third rate in its visual quality. Because our pupils are now daily in contact with graphics of a high standard through advertisements, television and magazines, their expectations about the visual quality of classroom material are, perhaps, higher than they used to be.

The layout and visual quality of a page is very important, probably more so than the content in motivating pupils to use the worksheet. The aim of this chapter is to show you that a great deal can be done to improve the visual quality of your material even though you may not have access to professional graphic design skills and even though you do not possess these skills yourself. The excuse 'but I can't draw' is not a valid one. First, the visual quality of a page does not rely on the presence of drawings or other illustrations. The general layout, the spacing, the choice of typeface, the use of headings and frames are equally important, and even a little thought given to these factors can make a big difference. Secondly, there are many kinds of simple graphics which a 'layman' can use.

Perhaps the most common fault is the page of unrelieved print. For most pupils, and particularly for the less able, this is daunting to look at, unmotivating and probably not the most effective way to put across whatever point you are trying to make. And the most common reasons behind this fault are first, a failure to think visually or to realize that there might be alternatives to presenting the information other than through the written word; and secondly, a belief on the part of the teacher that his or her task has ended once the information or tasks required have been set down in writing – the rest can be left to the typist.

However, considerations such as the layout of the page, the amount of information on the page, the juxtaposition of information/tasks/illustrations, and the continuity of format, are all very much part of the learning process and therefore very much the concern of the teacher who is producing the worksheet.

Spacing

Be clear what your worksheet is trying to achieve and then use horizontal and vertical spaces to convey this clearly to the learner. When used in a consistent way, spaces on the page can make the structure of the information or the task much more obvious. Figure 48 illustrates this point.

Figure 48(a) shows a page from a primary mathematics textbook. The criticisms that can be made of this page are as follows:

- In this figure the child first has to work *across* from left to right, doing 5(a), (b), (c) etc. and then 6(a), (b), (c) etc. He or she then works *down*, doing 1, 2, 3 etc.
- In answering questions 5 and 6 the child is likely to have difficulty in knowing exactly where he has got to because the sub-items (a),

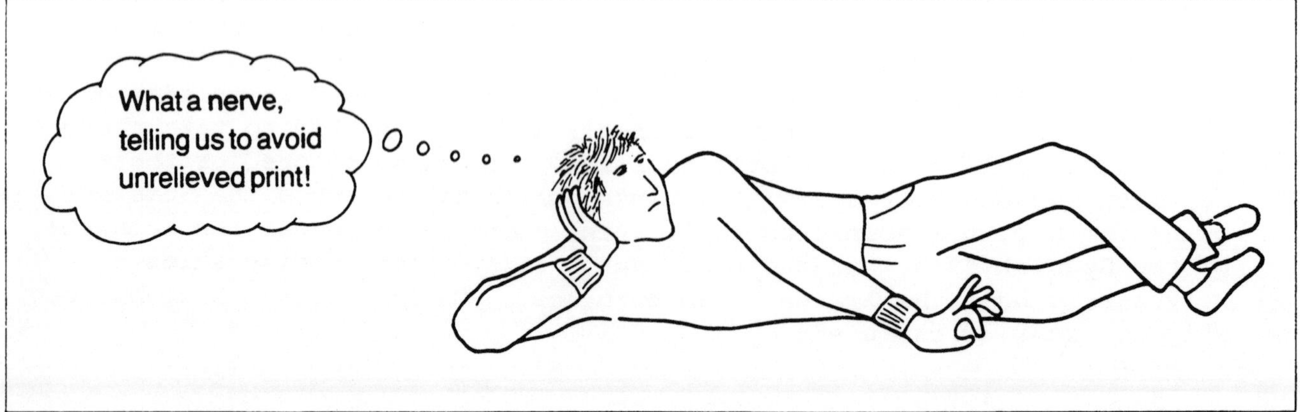

5 How much change should you get from 50p when you spend:
(a) 40p, (b) 20p, (c) 30p, (d) 10p, (e) 45p, (f) 25p, (g) 42p, (h) 38p, (i) 27p, (j) 34p, (k) 22p, (l) 17p?

1 Tom had 5p. He spent 3½p.
How much had he left?

2 Jim had 10p. He spent 4½p.
How much had he left?

3 Jean had 25p. She spent 6p on chocolate and 5p on sweets.
(a) How much did she spend?
(b) How much had she left?

4 John had 20p. He spent 9p on comics and 2p on sweets.
(a) How much did he spend?
(b) How much had he left?

6 How much change should you get from 100p when you spend:
(a) 50p, (b) 70p, (c) 80p, (d) 40p, (e) 95p, (f) 75p, (g) 45p, (h) 25p, (i) 42p, (j) 38p, (k) 58p, (l) 16p?

5 Anne went out with 30p. She spent 8p on cakes and 7p on lemonade.
(a) How much did she spend?
(b) How much had she left?

6 Shirley had 50p. She bought sweets for 12p and biscuits for 9p.
(a) How much did she spend?
(b) How much had she left?

Figure 48(a) *Using horizontal and vertical space*

(b) and (c) are not clearly differentiated from each other by space.

- The question indicators (1, 2, 3 etc.) are embedded in the text, and items 1, 2, 3 etc. are not differentiated from each other by appropriate spacing.

Figure 48(b) shows the same information redesigned with these points in mind.

Spaces between paragraphs, around diagrams or boxes and at page edges are important. If in doubt allow for more rather than less 'white space'. A simple uncluttered page makes for easier learning. A page which is too dense with information makes learning more difficult.

Typed work should normally be double spaced. Over-lengthy lines make for difficult reading. Sixty letters to the line should be the maximum.

Newspapers know what they are doing when they use short lines and several columns on a page. Using double columns is worth considering. It is also worth considering turning the page sideways to use triple columns. Human vision is horizontally, rather than vertically, orientated – TV screens, desks, slides and most pictures are in frames which are wider than they are tall.

Figure 49 (overleaf) shows the same passage of prose that was discussed in Chapter 8. Look at version A of the Armada passage in Chapter 8, and compare it with the version given here. Note the following points:

- The text has been divided into three columns, with a horizontal page format.
- Sub-headings have been given to the text. This not only makes it visually more acceptable, but also provides clues about the main point of each section, thereby aiding comprehension.
- Because the paragraphs are shorter and there are more of them, and because there are wider margins, there is more 'white space' in this version.

The general effect of the page is that it is less daunting, more inviting and 'user friendly'.

5 How much change should you get from 50p when you spend:

a	40p	e	45p	i	27p
b	20p	f	25p	j	34p
c	30p	g	42p	k	22p
d	10p	h	38p	l	17p

6 How much change should you get from 100p when you spend:

a	50p	e	95p	i	42p
b	70p	f	75p	j	38p
c	80p	g	45p	k	58p
d	40p	h	25p	l	16p

1 Tom had 5p. He spent 3½p. How much had he left?

2 Jim had 10p. He spent 4½p. How much had he left?

3 Jean had 25p. She spent 6p on chocolates and 5p on sweets.
a How much did she spend?
b How much had she left?

4 John had 20p. He spent 9p on comics and 2p on sweets.
a How much did he spend?
b How much had he left?

5 Anne went out with 30p. She spent 8p on cakes and 7p on lemonade.
a How much did she spend?
b How much had she left?

6 Shirley had 50p. She bought sweets for 12p and biscuits for 9p.
a How much did she spend?
b How much had she left?

Figure 48(b) *Using horizontal and vertical space*

THE ARMADA

A STORMY PASSAGE

Philip prepares for war

About 1585 Philip II seems to have decided to make a great attack on England.

Unlike Elizabeth, he possessed an army large enough to conquer a country. Even so he had to build or rather increase his fleet: the Mediterranean galleys which won the battle of Lepanto against the Turks were of little use in the stormy waters of the Channel or the wide Atlantic.

Philip's plan, as finally settled, was to land the Spanish army of the Netherlands in England under cover of a protecting fleet which would also carry a large force from Spain.

He expected, in view of reports from catholic exiles, that the English catholics would welcome him. In fact, most catholics would have fought against him as stoutly as they fought at sea, but it is Doubtful whether a united English resistance would have been strong enough to meet the best-trained army under the Duke of Parma, the first soldier of the age.

Fortunately for England, the test was not applied.

'Singeing King Philip's beard'

In April 1587, Drake sailed into Cadiz harbour to destroy many thousand tons of shipping and stores. Until the end of June, Drake's ships harassed all traffic along the coasts of the peninsular. Hence the Armada was not ready before the winter. The last preparations were not complete until May 1588, and the Spanish ships were not sighted off the Lizard until July 19th.

1588: The Armada sets sail

The Armada was an imposing sight, but half of it was made up of heavily laden transports and supply ships. In fighting strength the English were superior because their ships were faster, more easily handled, and built primarily as gun-carriers, whereas the Spanish ships, though heavily armed, still had the high superstructures designed for the old type of boarding warfare.

The English divided their forces: the western fleet – the larger of the two – was to prevent a direct landing, while the eastern fleet kept Parma from sending out his transports. The western fleet followed the Armada up the Channel, 'plucking their feathers', yet failing to break their unity.

The weakest point of Philip's plan, however, was the junction between the great fleet and Parma's transports. The transports could not come out unless they were protected from English attack; the nearest port deep enough to take the Armada was Flushing, and Flushing was in English and Dutch hands.

A disastrous defeat

In the afternoon of July 27th, the Armada anchored off Calais. About midnight on July 28th-29th the English, now joined by the eastern fleet, sent eight fireships against the Spaniards, and drove them out in confusion.

Next day, in a running fight along the coast towards Dunkirk, the range and weight of the English guns decided the issue. The Spanish Admiral could not turn back through the Channel; he was compelled to take the long course home round the British Isles. He had no pilots for these northern and western waters; the winds, which had favoured the Spanish plans in July, now completed their ruin.

Late in September the remnants of the Spanish fleet entered Santander. Sixty three Spanish ships – very nearly half the Armada – had been lost.

Figure 49 *The Armada again!*

Using lists
Lists of items, rather than sentences or paragraphs, are often easier for pupils to follow. Lists can be indented from the margin. If such lists do not need to be numbered or lettered for reference, it is better either to leave them unlabelled or to put dots or stars beside them for emphasis or for visual effect. For example

- This list is easier to assimilate than the paragraph above.
- Lists can be indented from the margin.
- Things need not be numbered unless it serves a purpose.
- Try putting dots or stars instead.

Try cutting up your material and laying it on one or more blank sheets. Then push the blocks of type, diagrams etc. about to form a more pleasing layout. Pasting can leave shadows when photocopying, so be sure to glue right up to the edges.

Using margins
In a good layout, the space between elements should always be less than the marginal widths, so think in terms of wide margins (see Figure 50).

It is not just a question of the amount of 'white space' and the amount of print on a page. The proportions and relationships between them are extremely important. Figure 51 overleaf shows how the margin at the bottom of the page should be greater than at the top. This figure also demonstrates that a double text page opening is taken as an entity and so the inner margins are less than the outer.

Finally, Figure 52 overleaf summarizes some useful guidelines on layout.

Lettering

The spacing of letters in a word is an important part of good lettering. Uniform mechanical spacing does not look right - optical spacing using your own judgement is better, as Figure 53 (p. 83) shows.

The space between words can be gauged by placing the letter 'O' from the alphabet in use between each word. The space between lines should be no less than the height of the small characters in use, as in Figure 54 (p. 83).

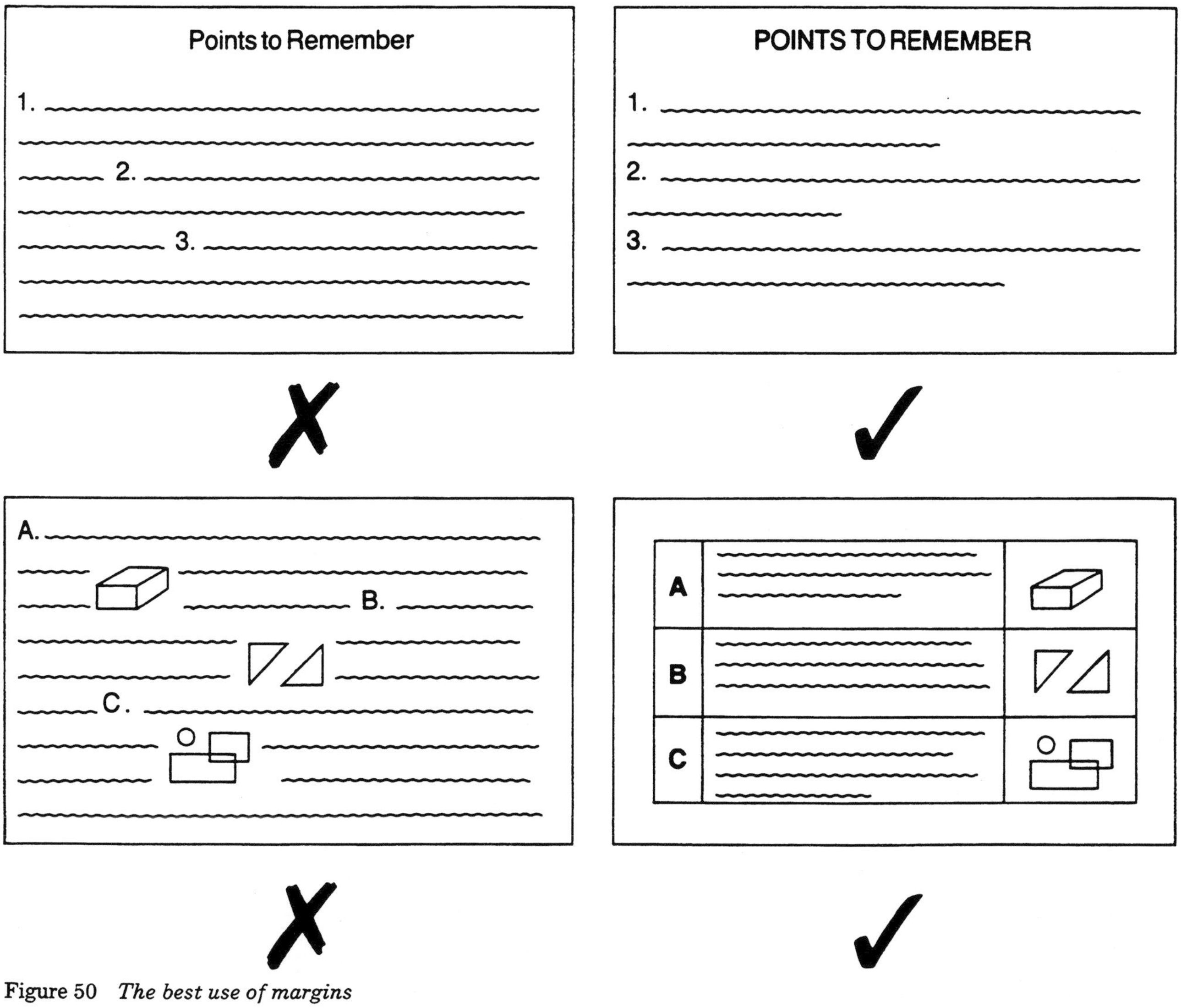

Figure 50 *The best use of margins*

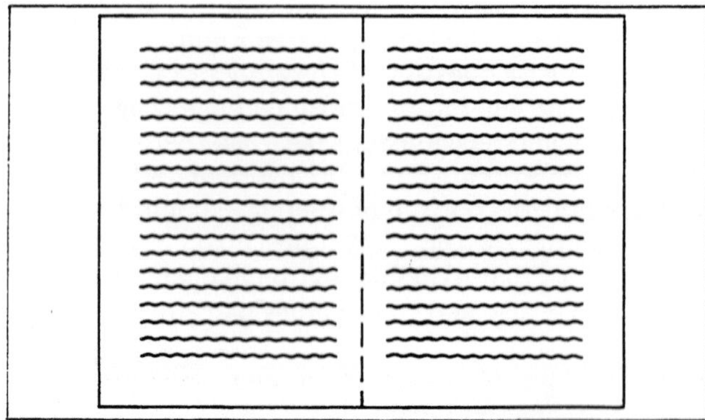

Figure 51 *Layout of a double page opening*

Dry transfer lettering
For headings and sub-headings a wide variety of styles and sizes of lettering is commercially available in the form of dry transfer lettering. Remember, however, that proliferation of different styles presents a cluttered and unnecessarily fussy appearance on the page (see Figure 55). Among the appropriate letter forms for clear presentation are Helvetica, Futura, Universe, Grotesque and Gill Serif.

Try to maintain some consistency about the styles of lettering used throughout your unit –

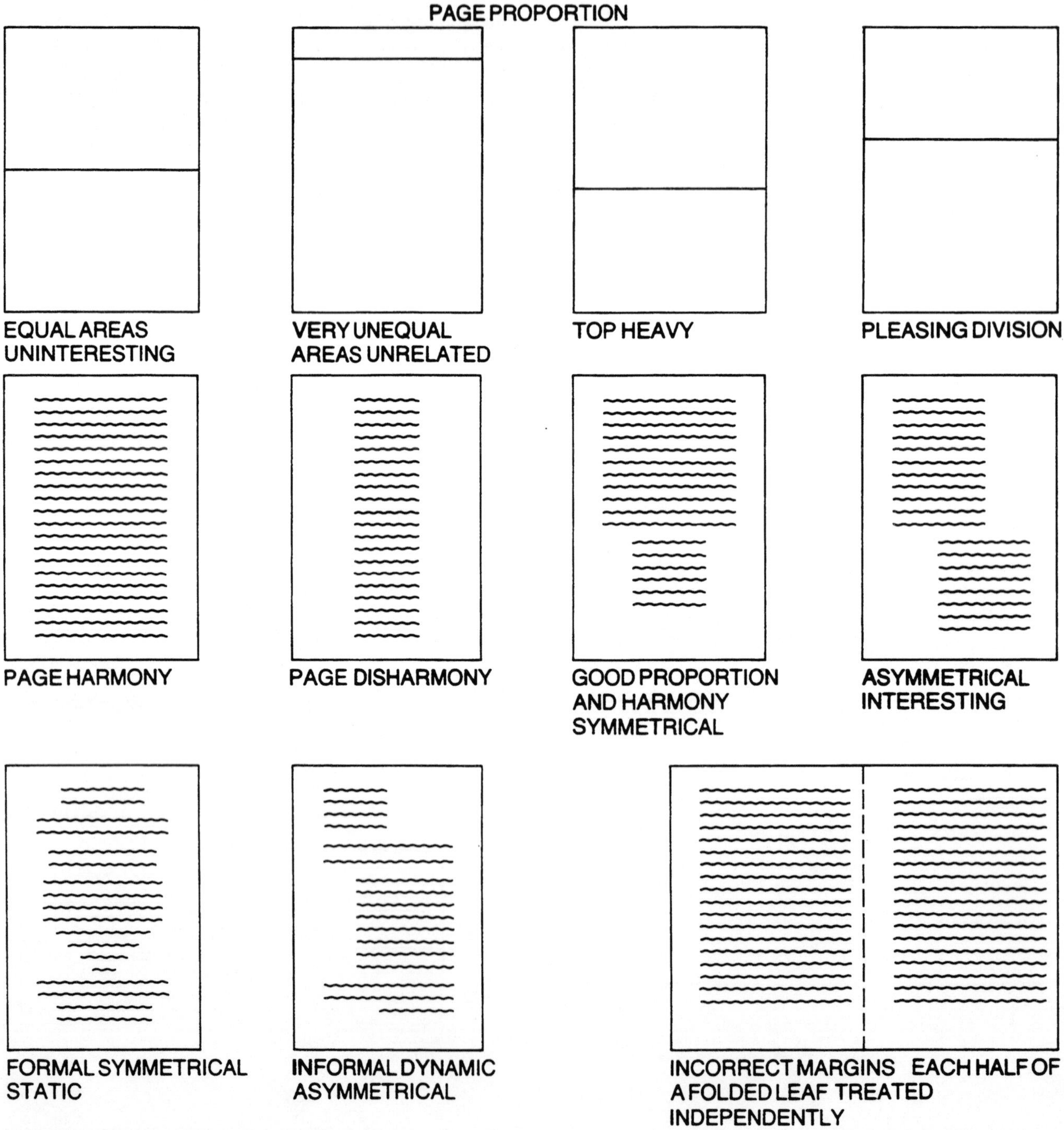

PAGE PROPORTION

EQUAL AREAS UNINTERESTING

VERY UNEQUAL AREAS UNRELATED

TOP HEAVY

PLEASING DIVISION

PAGE HARMONY

PAGE DISHARMONY

GOOD PROPORTION AND HARMONY SYMMETRICAL

ASYMMETRICAL INTERESTING

FORMAL SYMMETRICAL STATIC

INFORMAL DYNAMIC ASYMMETRICAL

INCORRECT MARGINS EACH HALF OF A FOLDED LEAF TREATED INDEPENDENTLY

Figure 52 *Some do's and don'ts of layout*

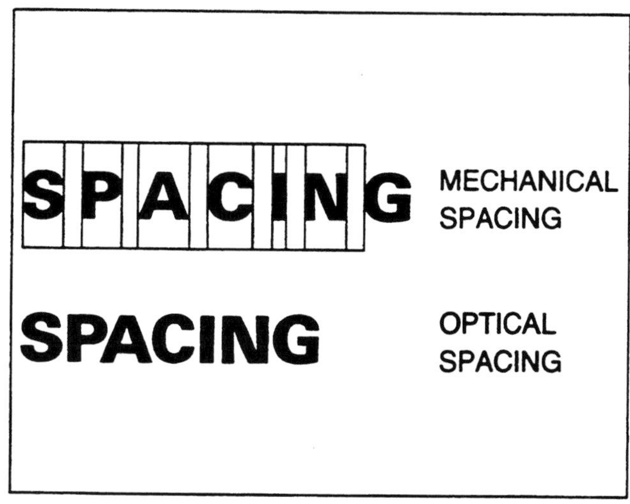

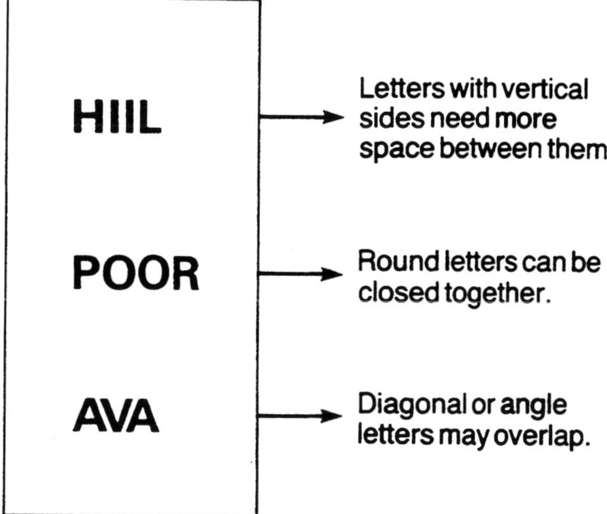

Figure 53 *Spacing the letters of a word*

e.g. main headings all in the same style, sub-headings in a uniform style.

Certain lettering sheets are available in colours as well as standard black and white, and transparent coloured lettering and symbols are produced for making overhead projection visuals and photographic transparencies.

To use dry transfer lettering, first remove the protective backing sheet and position the guide marks beneath the letter on a pre-drawn guide line. The sheet is then carefully burnished with a smooth instrument such as the cap of a ball-point pen. The letter is thus transferred to the artwork surface. When a line is completed, pencil guides can be erased carefully and lettering burnished (using the backing sheet again) for a firm adhesion. Completed lettering can then be protected by the application of a spray designed for this purpose. Always protect dry transfer sheets by storing them with the backing sheet in place.

Using dry transfer lettering can be time-consuming. However, certain words which will crop up again and again – e.g. Worksheet, Core, Extension, Text – need only be done once. Put your master copy on the page where you want it and photocopy the number of sheets you will need.

Theospaceobetweenowords
andolinesoofotype....

Figure 54 *Spaces between lines of lettering*

Typewritten text

Research has shown that any plain, clear typeface is easy to read. Italics or other fancy typefaces slow down reading and should be reserved for special uses such as emphasizing a word, a very important point, or highlighting instructions. Material printed entirely in capital letters is also slow to read.

If the typed matter is faint or irregular it will reproduce badly, and be difficult to read. So it is essential to persuade your typewriter to type sharply and in black, not grey. Keep the keys really clean, and try to use a machine in good condition.

It is best to use a carbon-ribbon electric typewriter. Carbon ribbons give a really clear black impression which reproduces well. Although they are expensive, lots of offices now have them and you should try to get the use of one.

'Golfball' typewriters have the characters on a single ball, so you can change the design of type, to italic for instance, simply by slotting on another ball. This means you can have different typefaces in different parts of the worksheet.

If a larger than normal type is required enquire about the availability of a Jumbo typewriter. Your school may not have one but a local Resource/ Teaching Centre might.

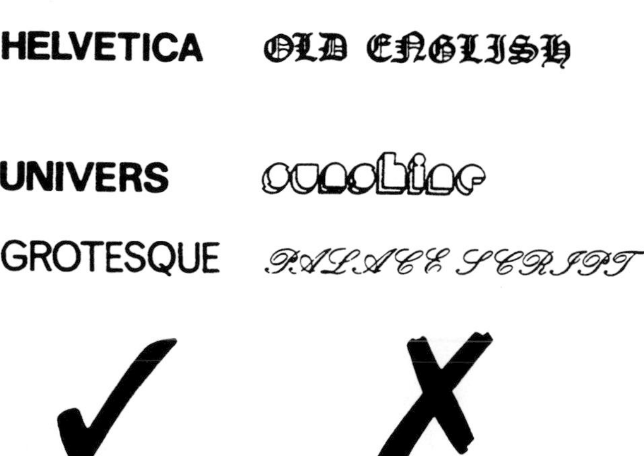

Figure 55 *Some examples of dry transfer lettering*

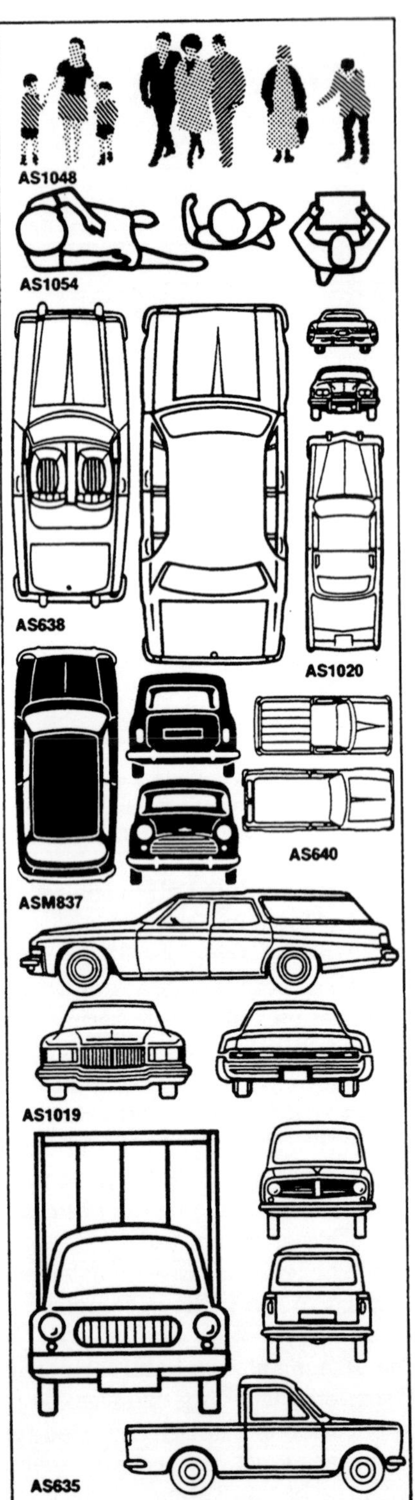

Figure 56 *Sheets of dry transfers (not to scale)*

Figure 57 *More dry transfers*

Use of boxes and frames

Framing the whole worksheet can make a startling difference to the overall visual impact. If you are planning to do this, don't redraw the frame for each sheet – do it once and photocopy the rest.

Boxes help keep different parts of your worksheet separate (i.e. diagrams, a wordbank, an activity as opposed to a piece of information). Numbers for headings, sections, questions etc. often look more attractive and less cold and formal if framed. However, beware of cluttering the page with too many frames.

If you want a fancier frame than a ruled one, here are some suggestions:

- Think about the possibilities with a typewriter – e.g. a frame made up of a string of the same letter or number or stars, dashes etc.
- Any Sunday newspaper contains advertisements in a whole variety of boxes and frames.
- A piece of blank paper, slightly smaller than a suitably selected book-cover, end-paper etc. would leave you with an attractive frame.
- A whole variety of lines, corners, curves etc. are available in dry transfer sheets.

'But I can't draw!'

Don't worry! For most worksheets you only need simple outlines of figures, buildings, vehicles etc. Here are some ideas for producing illustrations which are adequate for many learning situations.

Scissors and paste and an old textbook you don't mind cutting up provide probably the easiest way – but beware of infringing copyright.

Magazines, newspapers and mail-order catalogues are all sources of illustrations which can be traced to provide a simple outline. Using an acetate sheet and a black felt-tip pen is often easier than using paper and produces a better photocopy.

Many teachers accumulate collections of pictures which they think they might be able to use one day. However, in order to be able to use a picture when you want it, you must be able to find it. Some kind of cataloguing system is essential.

There are a number of copyright-free books on the market – e.g. the Graphics Ad Lib series (Business Books Ltd) and the Instant Art series (Graphic Books Ltd). These contain pictures of figures, faces, animals, machines, symbols, lettragraphics etc., all drawn in a simple black and white style easy for photocopying. Endless adaptations of these are possible by combining bits of pictures from different pages.

Sets of figures, trees, vehicles etc. are available on dry transfer sheets. Figures 56 and 57 (pp. 83 and 84) show samples of objects, figures and shadings available. Again, endless combinations of the individual items are possible.

Senior pupils with drawing skills are often delighted and flattered to be asked to help. You might even find an obliging parent.

If a larger version of a picture is needed, it can be projected on to a piece of paper by an episcope or an OHP. If you have access to a photocopier which has reduction and enlargement facilities, this too can be used to vary your basic drawings.

You may wish to photocopy only part of a picture from a book: either mask off the parts you don't want, or photocopy the whole picture, then cut out the bit you want. Sometimes a shadow-line appears when an image has been pasted into position and then copied. You can lose this by painting it out with white typewriter correcting fluid.

Half-tones (i.e. photographs) in newspapers don't photocopy well. However, satisfactory outlines can be obtained by outlining shapes and darkening some tones with a black felt-tip pen, and lightening others with white correcting fluid.

Two or three basic drawings can go much further than you think – they can be used in different roles in different parts of your unit. A simple figure can be multiplied to make a crowd, can be cut off for head and shoulders only, can be reduced or enlarged in scale, can undergo slight alterations.

More examples

Example 12
The worksheet in Figure 58 was produced in a workshop session in about twenty minutes by two teachers who claimed vehemently that they had no graphic skills at all. Notice the group of figures at the bottom of the sheet, used twice over; the tower is also used twice over. The worksheet is simple, uncluttered and well held together visually by the frame.

Perhaps the word 'worksheet' is too dominating. A logo or symbol might have been better, e.g.:

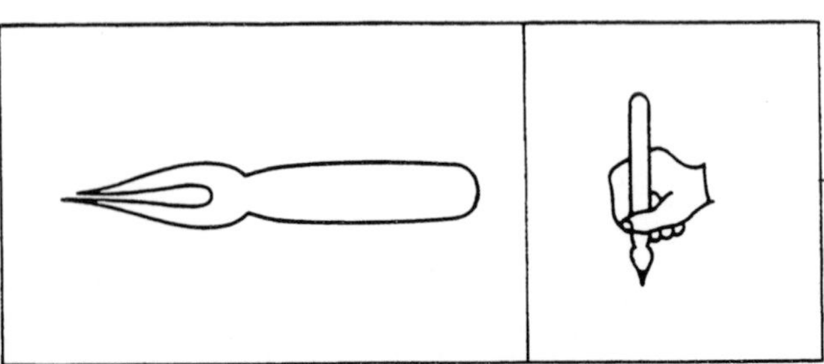

Example 13
'Cabinet Room', shown in Figure 59, p. 88, uses only two basic figures, both no more than simple outlines. The hands are very simply drawn and no faces are put on the forward-looking figures. This is

WORKSHEET 1

PARLIAMENT

LOOK AT THE DIAGRAM

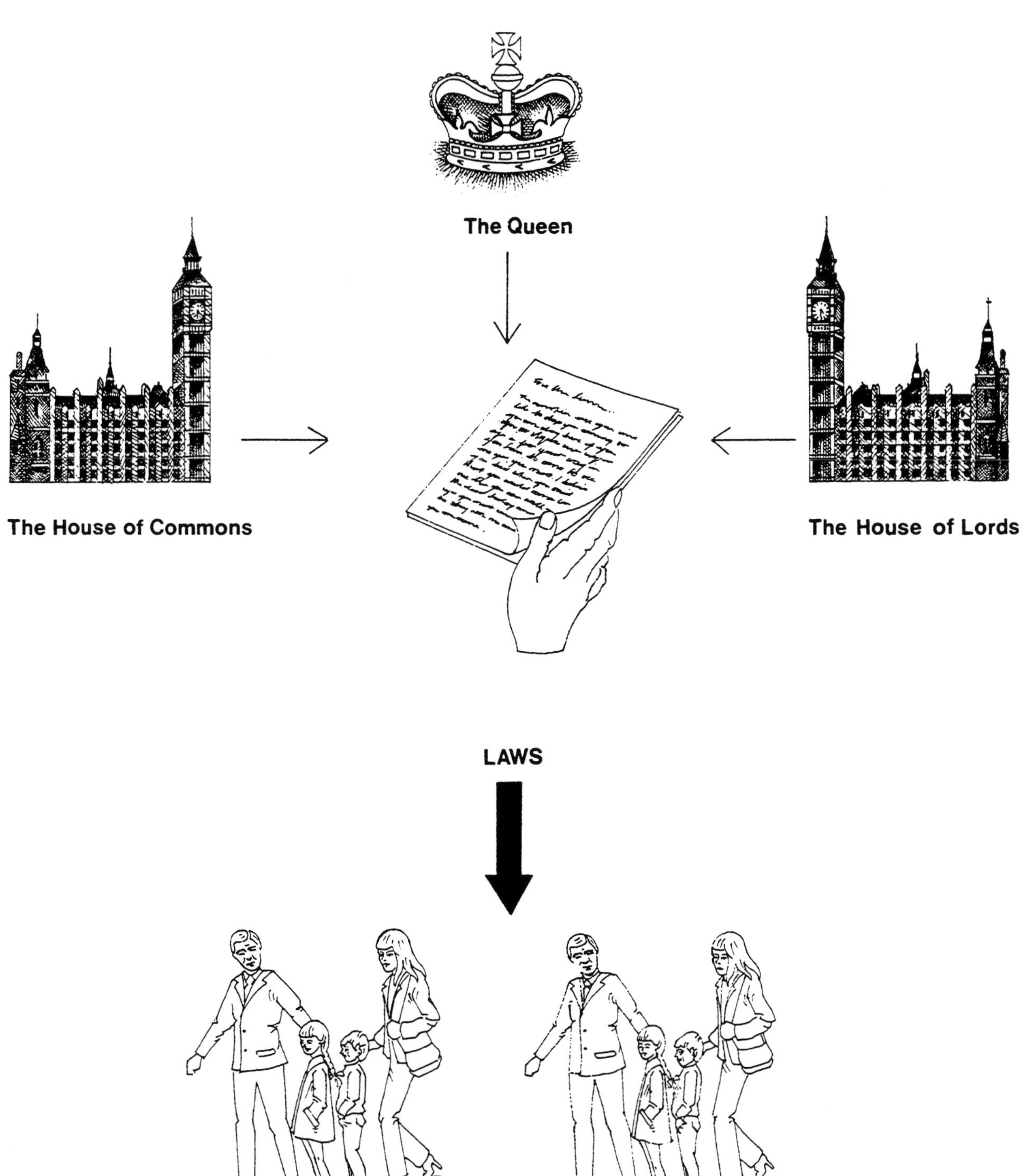

Figure 58 *Example 12*

CABINET ROOM

The Prime Minister and the Cabinet work together on all important areas affecting the country. Although there are often bitter arguments at these meetings they usually reach an agreement that all members of the Cabinet will support. This is called COLLECTIVE RESPONSIBILITY. If a Minister still disagrees and is unable to support the agreement he usually resigns.

Figure 59 *Example 13*

2. THE CRITIC

2.1 Asking questions: Literature

At frequent intervals during the course you have adopted the role of critic – of historical sources, paintings, music, or of an argument. Let us now look more closely at this process of criticism.

- On what criteria does the critic base his judgements?
- Does he back up his judgements by reference to passages from the text?

If you look back to Block 4, you will remember that Roger Lewis asked you to examine critically a passage from *Kes* – pages 24-26. I don't know whether you agreed with his comments on Hines' writing, but I hope you can see why he reached the conclusion he did. He first worked out what Hines was trying to do in this passage, and he thought that was to 'see the country as a source of positive values' in opposition to life on the housing estate. But Roger felt that the passage didn't succeed in establishing the countryside as an ideal. He found the writing too careful, too deliberately 'literary', too loaded with cliché. Notice the critic's sequence here:

- establishing the author's aim
- looking at the text in detail to see how far the aim is achieved
- quoting from the text to back up his argument

Look back to your discussion in Block 3 of Hines' characterisation of Mr Sugden and Mr Farthing. Maybe you felt that these characters were exaggerated, that Hines was constructing character types, caricatures even. If we are looking for complex and rounded characterisation in the novel, we have to admit *Kes*'s inadequacies here; it's not that kind of novel. In fact the use of caricature (e.g. Sugden) helps give this novel its impact. You might like to look at other passages in *Kes* where Barry Hines describes the rural scene or a character, to see whether Hines avoids the flaws of the passages discussed above.

I would like to look at another passage from the novel which is very different in aim and content and style from the rural description. It's an important extract, since it's the *ending* of the novel. I want to show *how* I make an assessment of its strengths and weaknesses: it's important to go beyond a mere expression of opinion when engaging in critical discussion. Please read the last 4½ pages of *Kes* starting on p. 156 'The Palace....'

Before you can make any assessment of the passage, you have to ask questions about it; questions about the author's intentions, his methods, his use of language. Make a list of questions you would like to ask about the passage and then compare it with mine.

My questions are as follows:

1. Why has Hines chosen a derelict cinema as the setting for this episode?
2. How does he describe the cinema? Is it easy to visualise?
3. What does Hines want to say about Billy's life, his feelings, his behaviour, in the passage?
4. Is this an appropriate way to end *Kes*?

Why did I ask these questions?

Figure 60 *Example 14*

Personal Checklist

FILL IN THE BLANK SPACES

I will be working at (Organization's name)..............................

(address)..

I must report to Mr/Mrs/Miss...

at (time)......am/pm on.......day, ...

Travel arrangements *(Check these with maps and timetables if necessary)*

I will have to leave home at .... (time) My fares will be ..... a day, and I will travel by ....

Suitable clothing and footwear (use the boxes below as a check list)

As I will be working in ....

I plan to wear ....

....

WORKPLACES, AND CONDITIONS
factory workshop garage office building or construction site library drawing office shop warehouse store hospital clinic standing sitting summer winter outdoors indoors clean dirty

TYPES OF CLOTHING AND FOOTWEAR
Smart clothes - collar and tie, blouse and skirt, makeup Working Clothes - jeans dungarees overalls boots anorak apron Protective clothing - gloves, waterproofs, wellingtons extra jersey cap

Eating arrangements

I will buy snacks at teabreaks and this will cost about .... each day.

I will need to take a packed lunch which I can eat at work or

I will be eating in the canteen/cafe and this will cost about .... each day.

Now add together

		£	p
Budget	Cost of travel per day	...	...
	Cost of food and extras per day	...	...
	Daily total	...	...

NOW FILL IN THE WORK EXPERIENCE APPLICATION FORM OPPOSITE

There are 2 copies

Copy 1. For your personal records. Use this one to practice.

Copy 2. For your 'employer'. Make sure that this is neat and all the details and spelling are correct.

☐ *Tick here when you have finished this paper*

Figure 61 *Example 15*

simple, effective and probably within the capability of most teachers (well, it certainly is now, because you can trace or photocopy these figures!).

Example 14
'The Critic' (Figure 60, p. 89) is a page entirely of prose with no illustrations, yet it is visually acceptable because of a well-planned layout. Note the use of a frame and wide margin; headings and sub-headings with different typefaces; key questions and points emphasized by black dots and extra spacing.

Example 15
In 'Personal Check List' (Figure 61, opposite) note the following points. All instructions are in a different typeface (italics). Hints and help about filling in the check list are provided. The use of boxes not only breaks up the print and is easier on the eye, but also keeps the actual check list separate from information and directions.

Examples 16 and 17
These show two ways of visually linking diagrams and instructional text, the former matching a block text with a block circuit diagram; the latter using parallel flowcharts (Figures 62 and 63).

Example 18
This example provides two suggestions for different ways of framing or boxing a piece of information (Figure 64, p. 93).

Example 19
This example refers to Case study 4 in Chapter 3 – the 'Protest' worksheets. Comments on the general visual quality of these follow (p.94).

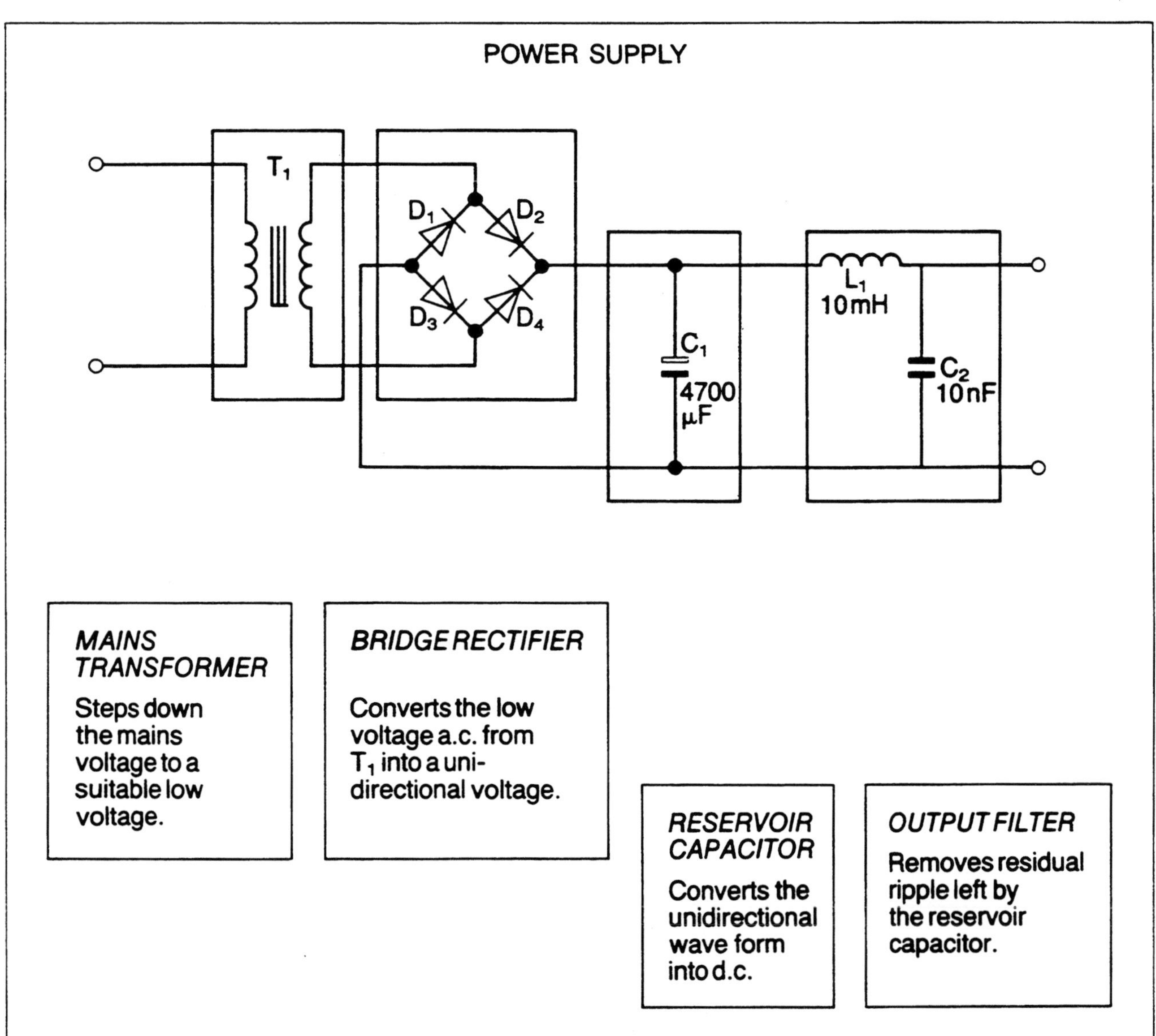

Figure 62 *Example 16*

INFORMATION PRESENTED IN FLOWCHARTS

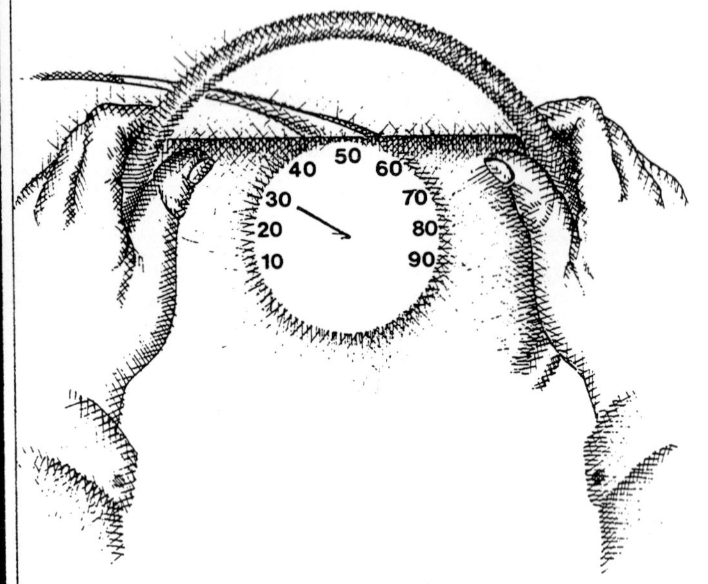

Look at the speed of the car.

Speed = **30** miles per hour.

A flowchart can be used to find the stopping distance.

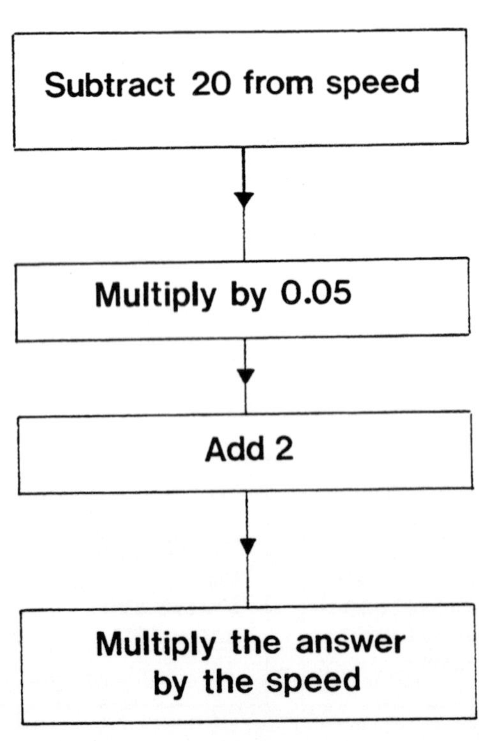

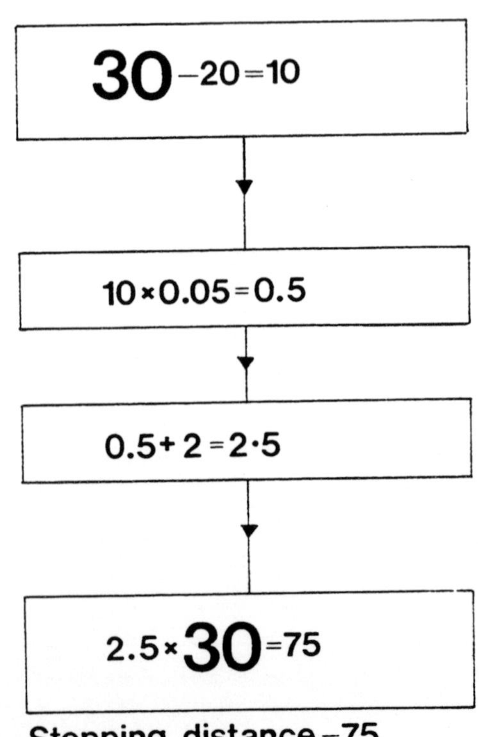

Figure 63 *Example 17*

Textbooks have certain drawbacks in that they cannot closely reflect the interests and ability levels of your pupils; and marketing considerations make it difficult to pitch a book entirely at one particular teaching strategy, mode of assessment or syllabus. However, textbooks do have the great advantage of being professionally printed, with professionally produced graphics and facilities for colour plates etc. On the other hand, teacher-produced material, while being geared to the specific needs of particular children and reflecting current educational thinking, is often amateur in its production and sometimes third-rate in its visual quality. Because our pupils are now daily in contact with graphics of a high standard through advertisements, television, magazines, etc, their expectations about the visual quality of classroom material are, perhaps, higher than they used to be.

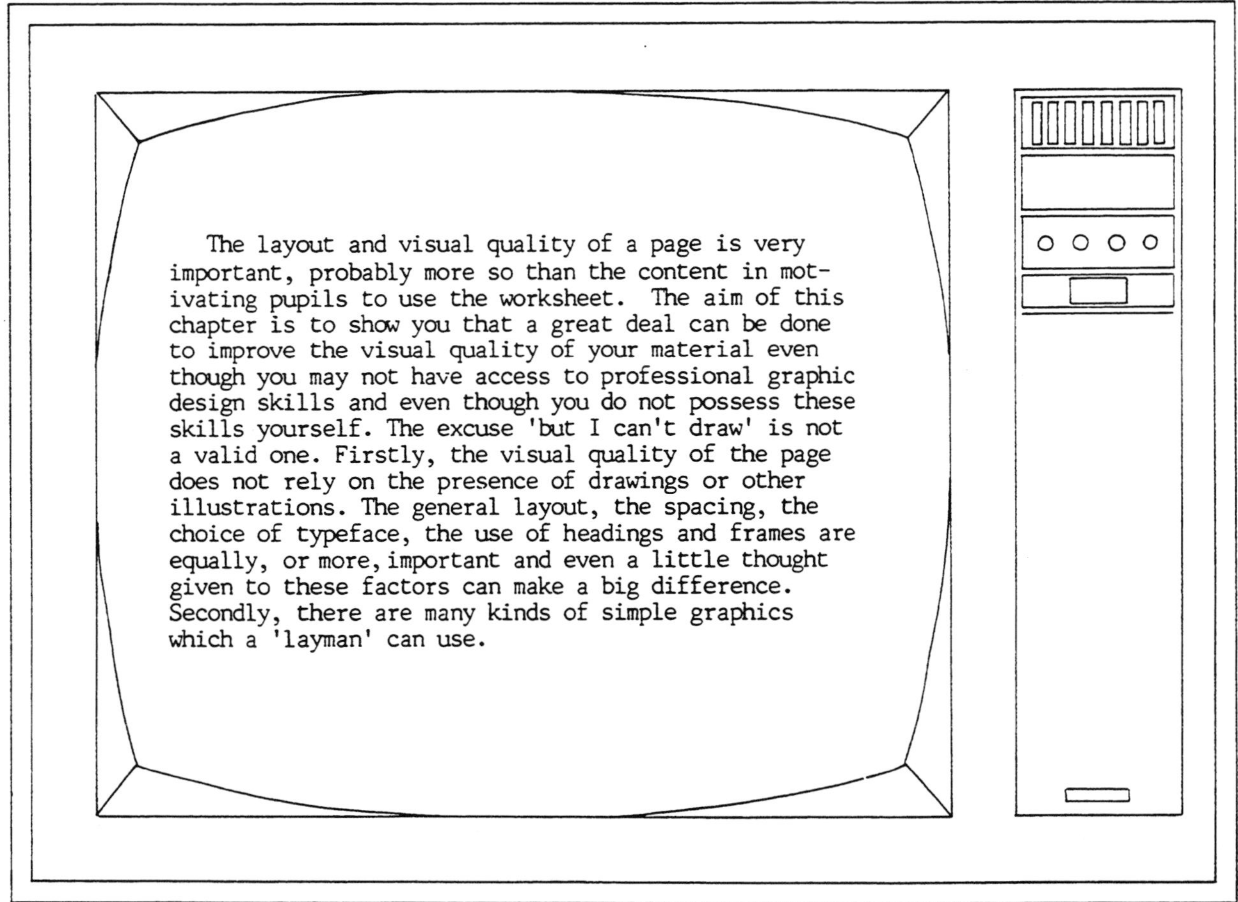

The layout and visual quality of a page is very important, probably more so than the content in motivating pupils to use the worksheet. The aim of this chapter is to show you that a great deal can be done to improve the visual quality of your material even though you may not have access to professional graphic design skills and even though you do not possess these skills yourself. The excuse 'but I can't draw' is not a valid one. Firstly, the visual quality of the page does not rely on the presence of drawings or other illustrations. The general layout, the spacing, the choice of typeface, the use of headings and frames are equally, or more, important and even a little thought given to these factors can make a big difference. Secondly, there are many kinds of simple graphics which a 'layman' can use.

Figure 64 *Example 18*

The general layout is reasonably motivating, being well spaced and no areas of text being too overwhelming. However, attention to the following details would have improved the visual quality:

- adherance to the rule that margins should be wider than any other space on the page;
- a frame round each sheet;
- some distinction between the general text and the exercises – e.g. use of italics, boxes, a symbol at the side;
- in exercise 18 (design a placard and a badge), more space was needed, the badge was far too small to do anything worth while, and some pupils might need guidance on what to draw.

The cartoon about pressure groups is simple and effective and there is nothing here which couldn't have been drawn by any teacher.

More suggestions

Worksheets sometimes benefit from the use of a logo or symbol. For example, instead of printing 'Worksheet', 'Information sheet', 'Activity' at the head of each page or section, you could use a logo or symbol throughout your unit.

Colour printing is seldom available to teachers, but there are possibilities in asking pupils to colour illustrations for themselves. You must use your judgement, of course, about when this is an educational activity and when it is merely a 'keep them quiet' activity. Colour can also be introduced by using coloured paper or card for the actual worksheets.

If worksheets are of the kind which are filled in and kept by the pupils, blanks or framed spaces can be left for pupils to draw their own pictures or diagrams. Various degrees of guidance can be given in pupil-constructed graphics.

Diagrams, charts and illustrations give visual variety to the page. However, this alone should not be a reason for including them. They must be appropriate and a better form of teaching/learning device than some other alternatives.

Some do's and don'ts when using illustrations

- Don't be tempted to cram too much information into one graphic. A series of graphics, building up the information step by step, would be a more effective learning aid and visually more acceptable.
- Do put your illustration, graph, example etc. in the right place and sequence in the text.
- Don't place your illustration so that the reader has constantly to turn the page to refer to it.
- Give your illustration a clear caption. If a different kind of lettering or type is used for this, make sure it is consistent throughout the unit.
- In drawing up tables, don't draw vertical lines if you want the eye to travel horizontally, and vice versa.

Chapter Ten

A question of form

Forms and questionnaires are often associated with worksheets - e.g. a survey conducted by the pupils about some aspect of the local community, a questionnaire about themselves, a form designed to help evaluate the course they have done.

This brief chapter gives a few hints about the planning and design of questionnaires.

Design factors

A common fault in the design of forms is the overuse of ruled lines. This can be off-putting. Leaving spaces instead of lines is much better. Another fault is to leave inadequate space for answering questions.

The best designed forms or questionnaires are those which are:

- quickest to type;
- cheapest to produce;
- easiest to fill in;
- not confusing or ambiguous and give the most accurate information;
- quickest and most convenient to code and analyse.

Unfortunately these are sometimes conflicting requirements. It is up to you to decide the priorities.

Look at Figure 65. Version A was much easier to type than C because the former is lined up from the left-hand margin, whereas with the latter the typist has to calculate back from the right-hand margin before knowing where to begin. Version B is the most difficult to code and analyze because the numbers and the response boxes are separated and because the boxes are not in line. Of course in such a short example the difference is small; but multiply both the number of questions and the number of replies and the time difference becomes significant.

Figure 66 overleaf shows different ways of indicating a choice between alternatives. Versions A and B are probably the most suitable. Version C might be used if the list was fairly expansive and too unwieldy to present in formats A or B. Version D is not suitable - negative questions should be avoided and deletions reserved for limited choices (e.g. Mr/Mrs/Miss).

A If the old church in the High Street was pulled down, I would feel:

1. ☐ very sorry
2. ☐ sorry
3. ☐ don't know
4. ☐ pleased
5. ☐ very pleased

B If the old church in the High Street was pulled down, I would feel:

1. very sorry ☐
2. sorry ☐
3. don't know ☐
4. pleased ☐
5. very pleased ☐

C If the old church in the High Street was pulled down, I would feel:

very sorry ☐ 1
sorry ☐ 2
don't know ☐ 3
pleased ☐ 4
very pleased ☐ 5

Figure 65 *Various designs for the same multiple-choice question*

Unless the place for putting a cross or tick is specified, errors can arise in relating the entry to the caption, as shown in Figure 67 overleaf.

Mixed methods of indicating a choice on the same form can be confusing or can cause errors in completion. A change in method should be avoided, especially if it involves a reversal of thought for the person completing the form. Never mix on the same form a positive type of entry (e.g. by a tick) with the negative one of deleting alternative words and phrases. Figure 68, p. 97 is a model you should *not* follow!

A difficulty often encountered in designing forms and questionnaires is that of fitting headings or explanations of responses required into narrow columns or margins. Sometimes it can be done by fitting the print in vertically, but this is annoying to the reader. Figure 69, p. 97 shows some ways of overcoming the problem.

The questions you ask

A survey can never be better than its questionnaire. If you ask ambiguous, vague and

A.

Put a ring round the day of the week you would be available for team practice.

Monday, Tuesday, Wednesday, Thursday, Friday

B.

Put a tick in the box opposite the day of the week you could come to team practice.

Monday ☐
Tuesday ☐
Wednesday ☐
Thursday ☐
Friday ☐

C.

Which day of the week can you come to team practice? ....

D.

Delete which days you cannot come to team practice.

Monday/ Tuesday/ Wednesday/ Thursday/ Friday

Figure 66 *Various ways of indicating a choice between alternatives* (*source: Design of Forms*, HMSO, 1972)

BAD

Place a cross against the items for which a claim is being made:

Loss of equipment ✗ Equipment replaced
Equipment repairs Hire of equipment

GOOD

Place an X against the items for which a claim is being made:

Loss of equipment ☐ Equipment replaced ☒
Equipment repairs ☐ Hire of equipment ☐

(b) Captions should be placed close to a box to avoid confusion and errors.

BAD

Goods to be sent by (insert X in appropriate box)

☐ Road ☐ Rail ☒ Sea ☐ Air

GOOD

Goods to be sent by (insert X in appropriate box)

Road ☐ Rail ☐ Sea ☒ Air ☐

Figure 67 *Good and bad arrangements for indicating a choice* (*source: Design of Forms*, HMSO, 1972)

irrelevant questions you will get ambiguous, vague and irrelevant answers. Think also about the order in which you ask questions. Questions like 'Are you over 18?' should come *before* a question like 'Did you vote in the last General Election?'

Try to avoid leading questions or questions which will influence an answer: 'You don't really think . . . do you?' is hardly impartial!

Try to avoid questions where there is a possibility of an inaccurate answer, or where people

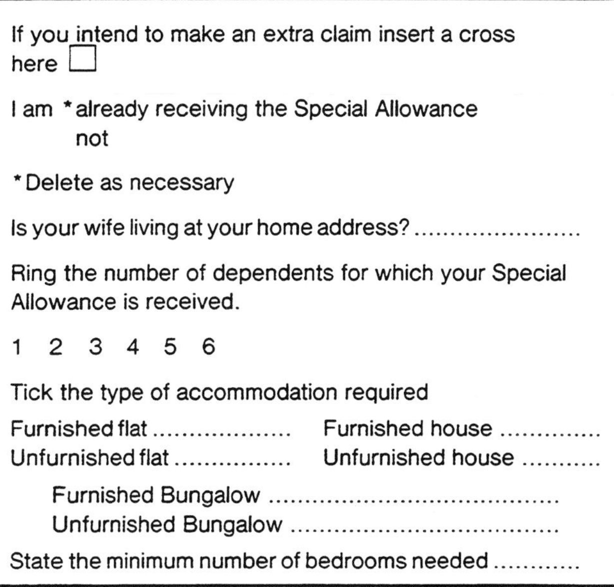

If you intend to make an extra claim insert a cross here ☐

I am *already receiving the Special Allowance
not

*Delete as necessary

Is your wife living at your home address? ....

Ring the number of dependents for which your Special Allowance is received.

1 2 3 4 5 6

Tick the type of accommodation required

Furnished flat .... Furnished house ....
Unfurnished flat .... Unfurnished house ....

Furnished Bungalow ....
Unfurnished Bungalow ....

State the minimum number of bedrooms needed ....

Figure 68 *An example of a badly designed form* (*source*: *Design of Forms*, HMSO, 1972)

will make up an answer – e.g. relying on faulty memory, or not wanting to admit ignorance.

Avoid asking a long, complex question – break it down into several simpler questions. And do not have double-barrelled questions – e.g. 'Do you like travelling on trains and buses?'

Opinions held by people are often multi-faceted. A question asked in one way will get a different aspect of the person's opinion than if it was asked in another way. Asking for opinions is very difficult, but measuring *attitudes* is a little easier. For example, instead of 'What do you think about capital punishment?' make a statement with which the respondant can agree or disagree:

'I think capital punishment should be abolished.'

I agree strongly with this statement. ☐
I agree, but with reservations. ☐
I haven't made up my mind yet. ☐
I disagree, but with reservations. ☐
I disagree strongly. ☐

Always try out your questionnaire on a few 'guinea-pigs' before using it for real. You will be the last person to spot your own ambiguities!

More essential groundwork

If your pupils are conducting a survey outside the school there are other things to think of as well as the questions they are going to ask. If, for example, they are doing a survey in the local shopping centre, have you:

- checked that a similar survey has not been conducted recently by some other organization? Although a repeat will have educational value for your pupils, this is not good public relations;

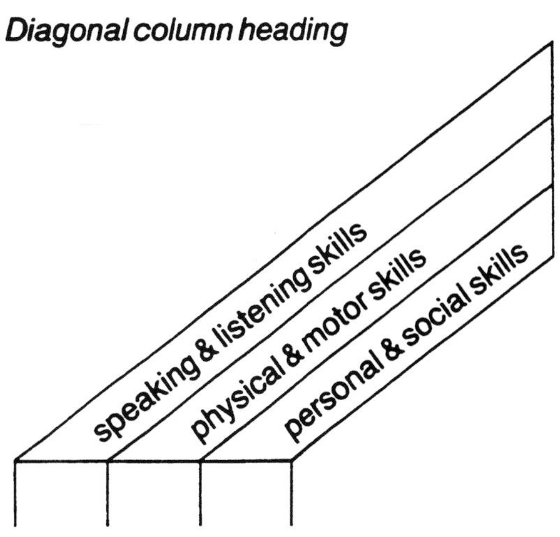

Overlapping heading

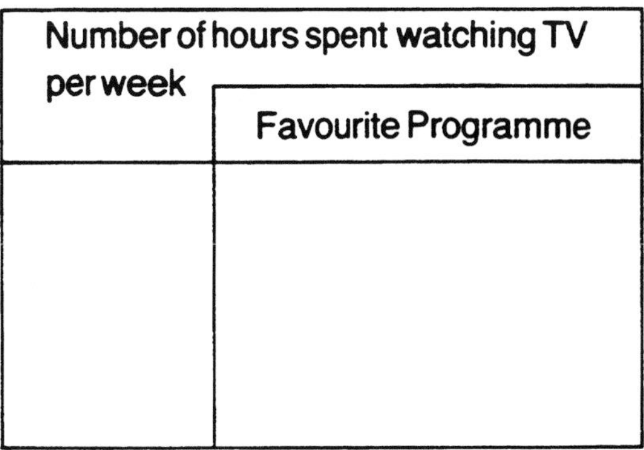

Use of arrows

My Knowledge/Skills:

I think my knowledge and skills have shown –

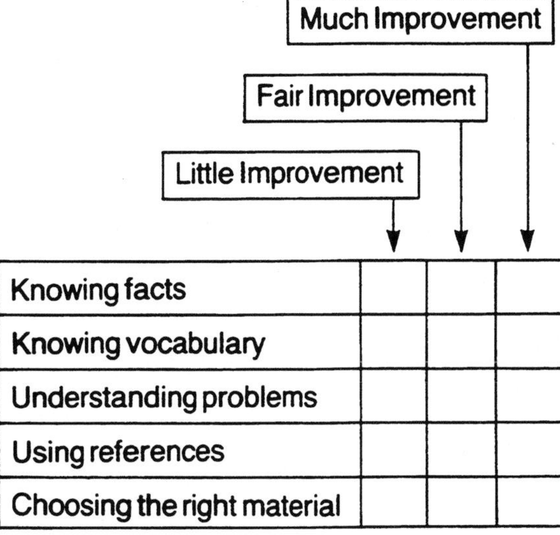

Figure 69 *Various ways of fitting column headings*

- made sure that the insurance situation is covered;
- briefed your pupils about how to get there, e.g. safety in crossing roads etc.;
- rehearsed your pupils in how to ask the questions, saying 'thank you' etc.;
- informed shopkeepers of the project and gained their approval;
- given each pupil a letter to carry in case anyone challenges his authority. The letter should state the purpose of the survey and ask for cooperation;
- thought about the effects of rain, wind etc. - i.e. provided clip-boards and plastic envelopes?

Case study 15

This is a study of a questionnaire used with the in-service education material *Education for Family Life: a Planning Pack for Teachers* (Open University, 1981), which was produced by the OU in association with the Health Education Council.

The purpose of the questionnaire was to help teachers assess more clearly where the interests of young people lie within a range of themes related to health.

A questionnaire such as that shown in Figure 70, opposite, was used in conjunction with a similar questionnaire for parents. The functions of these two questionnaires were seen as follows:

- Staff can plan course work for particular classes in the knowledge of the pupils' interests. This will help to ensure that content is relevant to all pupils.
- Differences in attitudes between boys and girls are discovered. (Some may be predicted, but others can be unexpected.)
- Differences in stages of development of the pupils can be observed.
- The effects of school courses and influences outside school are suggested.
- The differences and similarities between parents, teachers and pupils in their perceptions of the importance of the topics can be considered. From this platform of knowledge, decisions on curriculum content in these most important areas can be made with the confidence of having consulted those most concerned.
- Senior staff, having been informed of the attitudes of parents, teachers and children with regard to these topics, are placed in a strong position, if challenged, regarding curriculum decisions in these important and sometimes sensitive areas.

There may be occasions when, instead of being on the asking end of a questionnaire or survey, you want your pupils to be on the receiving end. For example, you may wish to discover where their interests lie, how certain topics are perceived by them, what their attitudes are about certain issues. Case study 15 shows a part of one such questionnaire for pupils.

Sometimes it is a useful preliminary exercise to prepare your pupils for a questionnaire by putting a mini-questionnaire of the same structure (but different topics) on the blackboard and asking pupils to jot down their responses. They then discuss what they mean by 'High' or 'Low' interest etc.

It may also be important to point out that their responses are anonymous or that there is no right or wrong answer. What each individual feels is what is wanted, not necessarily what their friends think, nor what they think is expected by you.

In addition to providing you with useful information for planning, for getting to know your pupils etc, questionnaires of this type can also be a teaching tool, stimulating discussion about how the pupils responded, why they thought one thing rather than another, what questions might have been asked which weren't.

Processing the information

The information for each topic is first transferred to summary sheets (an example is shown in Figure 71(a), p. 99). Note the useful way of counting the ten responses in the low-interest column - in batches of five (four strokes, with the fifth stroke diagonally cancelling the batch).

The numbers of responses are then weighted according to which column they are in - e.g. high × 3, medium × 2, low × 1, nil × 0 (Figure 71(b), p. 99, and the total number of points is then added up for each topic (Figure 71(c)).

Health topic questionnaire for pupils

male m ☐ f ☐ female age class/form

Listed below are twenty-eight topics to do with health. We want to know which of these topics you think are important to learn about in school. Please think about each topic and then put a tick in the box to show if your interest is HIGH, MEDIUM, LOW or NIL. If you tick the HIGH box, then you are very interested in that topic and would like to see it covered in school. MEDIUM means that you are interested, but don't think that it's so important to cover it. LOW means you are not very interested but wouldn't mind covering it, and NIL means that you don't want to cover that topic.

When you have finished choose the three topics that you think are the most important. Write the numbers of these topics in the 1st, 2nd and 3rd choice boxes opposite. ***Thank you for your co-operation.***

1ST CHOICE	2ND CHOICE	3RD CHOICE

TOPIC	INTEREST LEVEL (tick one box for each topic) HIGH	MEDIUM	LOW	NIL
1. Health services (doctors, dentists, hospitals, etc.)	☐	☐	☐	☐
2. Safety in the home	☐	☐	☐	☐
3. Drinking alcohol	☐	☐	☐	☐
4. Handicapped people	☐	☐	☐	☐
5. Sex	☐	☐	☐	☐
6. Conservation (protecting trees, animals, etc.)	☐	☐	☐	☐
7. First Aid	☐	☐	☐	☐
8. Nutrition (how food affects your health)	☐	☐	☐	☐
9. Venereal disease (VD)	☐	☐	☐	☐
10. Control of body weight	☐	☐	☐	☐
11. Cancer	☐	☐	☐	☐
12. Using leisure time	☐	☐	☐	☐
13. Road safety	☐	☐	☐	☐
14. Water safety	☐	☐	☐	☐
15. Growth and development (of a young person becoming an adult)	☐	☐	☐	☐
16. Morality (the difference between right and wrong)	☐	☐	☐	☐
17. Personal hygiene	☐	☐	☐	☐
18. Care of very young children	☐	☐	☐	☐
19. Personal relationships (getting on with other people)	☐	☐	☐	☐
20. Taking drugs	☐	☐	☐	☐
21. Contraception (birth control)	☐	☐	☐	☐
22. Exercise and health	☐	☐	☐	☐
23. Smoking	☐	☐	☐	☐
24. Mental health (health of the mind)	☐	☐	☐	☐
25. Pollution	☐	☐	☐	☐
26. The internal organs of the human body (and how they work)	☐	☐	☐	☐
27. Dental health	☐	☐	☐	☐
28. Common diseases that can be caught from other people	☐	☐	☐	☐

Figure 70 *Case study 15*

Health topic survey Summary sheet 1m

Number of completed questionnaires 16

age of pupils 15.2 – 16.1

class/form 4C

TOPICS	INTEREST LEVEL TALLIES				IMPORTANCE TALLIES		
	HIGH	MEDIUM	LOW	NIL	FIRST	SECOND	THIRD
1. Health services	(0)	IIII (4)	HHH HHH (10)	II (2)	(0)	(0)	(0)

Figure 71(a) *Case study 15 – processing of information*

Health topic survey Summary sheet 2m

Number of completed questionnaires 16

age of pupils 15.2 – 16.1

class/form 4C

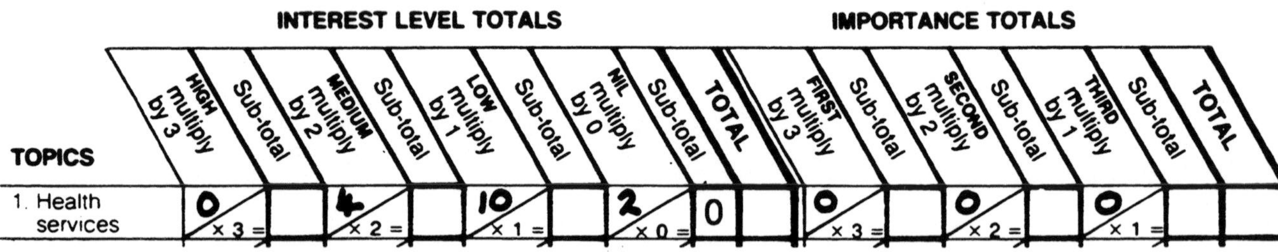

TOPICS	INTEREST LEVEL TOTALS									IMPORTANCE TOTALS						
	HIGH multiply by 3	Sub-total	MEDIUM multiply by 2	Sub-total	LOW multiply by 1	Sub-total	NIL multiply by 0	Sub-total	TOTAL	FIRST multiply by 3	Sub-total	SECOND multiply by 2	Sub-total	THIRD multiply by 1	Sub-total	TOTAL
1. Health services	0 × 3 =		4 × 2 =		10 × 1 =		2 × 0 =	0		0 × 3 =		0 × 2 =		0 × 1 =		

Figure 71(b) *Case study 15 – processing of information*

Health topic survey Summary sheet 2m

Number of completed questionnaires 16

age of pupils 15.2 – 16.1

class/form 4C

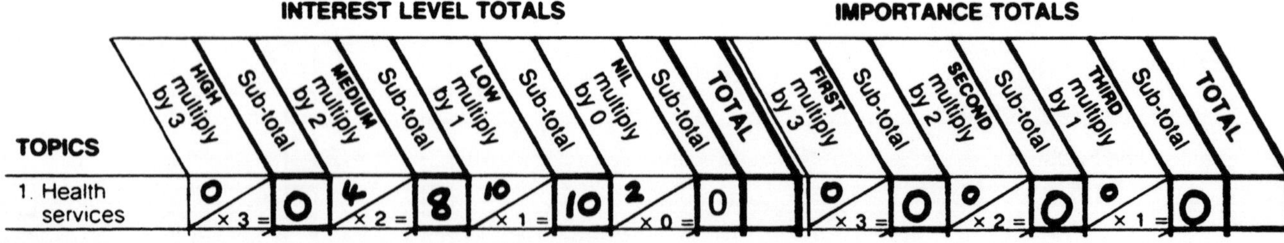

TOPICS	INTEREST LEVEL TOTALS									IMPORTANCE TOTALS						
	HIGH multiply by 3	Sub-total	MEDIUM multiply by 2	Sub-total	LOW multiply by 1	Sub-total	NIL multiply by 0	Sub-total	TOTAL	FIRST multiply by 3	Sub-total	SECOND multiply by 2	Sub-total	THIRD multiply by 1	Sub-total	TOTAL
1. Health services	0 × 3 =	0	4 × 2 =	8	10 × 1 =	10	2 × 0 =	0		0 × 3 =	0	0 × 2 =	0	0 × 1 =	0	

Figure 71(c) *Case study 15 – processing of information*

Chapter Eleven

To arrive is better than to travel hopefully

This chapter is about evaluation of learning materials. Much of the literature of evaluation has been concerned with large-scale projects, conducted at a daunting level of sophistication and statistical complexity. This chapter is comparatively humble, being concerned with what teachers can do to evaluate their own materials in their own schools or local working parties.

Two points central to this chapter are:

- Evaluation is a process of deciding what educational outcomes you desire and expect and comparing them with what actually happens.
- The purpose of evaluation is to provide information for decision making - decisions about whether and how to change your material, your methods, your aims etc.

It must be emphasized, however, that points such as these cover only a fraction of the controversial and expanding field of evaluation. This chapter takes only a brief glimpse at some aspects of column A and some aspects of column C of Table 12.

Table 12
Table comparing three major types of evaluation

1	*Symbol*	*A*	*B*	*C*
2	Type or model	Behavioural/Specific Objectives. Quantitative. Engineering model.	'Goal Free'. Social Morality. Comprehensive Rational.	Qualitative. Humanistic. Responsive. Illuminative. Transactional.
3	Author(s) or representatives	R Tyler	M Scriven	R Stake M Parlett and D Hamilton
4	Aims	Measure learners' and instructors' progress towards specified objectives. Increase productivity and accountability.	Assess the effects and the objectives of the programme. Inform and educate public to choose more rationally.	Report the different ways in which a programme is seen and judged. Understand diversity.
5	Key questions	Are teachers efficient? Are learners mastering objectives efficiently?	What are all the effects? Do they match rationally justifiable wants of all participants?	How does the programme appear to different people? What are the different stories being told?
6	Advantages	Quantitative record of teachers' and learners' progress. Responsibility for learners' progress.	Freedom from rhetoric of intent. Independent criticism of pressure-group bias.	Broad view of variety of expectations and processes.
7	Disadvantages	Neglect of unintentional results and interpersonal processes. 'If you can't test it, don't teach it.'	High dependence on record-keeping and documentation. High demands on rationality of consumers and evaluators.	Low generalizability. Tendencies towards subjectivism or relativism.
8	Methodology	Pre and post tests. Task analysis. Objective, criterion - referenced testing. Discrimination indices.	Bias control through use of check-list and argument. Commitment to standards.	Case-studies. Participant - observation. Interviews. Legal drama.
9	Typical forms of expertise	Objectives writers. Measurement specialists. Statistical skills.	Quasi-legal (Arguments for and against) Philosophical 'crap-detection'.	Journalistic. Historical. Sociological. Anthropological.
10	Background	Scientific Management Movement. Bureaucracy. Agricultural-botany.	Philosophy applied to important questions of life.	Anti-scientism trends. Humanities. Divergent thinking.

Source: Evaluation in Education, unit in Learning Resources Department, Dundee College of Education 1979

Formative evaluation

In keeping with the title of this book, the discussion in the following pages is mostly about formative evaluation – that is, not a summing up and judgement of your course once it is finished (summative evaluation), but a process that is on-going, providing feedback about your material, methods and organization in the developmental stages, and thus being part of the formative process.

As Figure 72 shows, formative evaluation is an integral part of the design and development of any course or unit. This, however, is a model, not reality. Rather than being a clear sequence, the whole process is much more interactive than the diagram suggests. Consideration of content is seldom delayed so long. It is a circular process and, provided the full circle is travelled, the entry point is less important than some theorists would have it.

Analysis of the situation

- Diagnosis of the problem – why are you producing new material and writing new worksheets; to what situation or problem is this a response?
- What are the major constraints within which you are operating – e.g. ability of the pupils; resources available; ability and aptitudes of the teachers who will be using the material (including yourself); timetabling constraints?
- The wider context and the wider questions – how does what you are planning to do fit in with broader educational aims; is what you are planning better than what it is replacing; what is your definition of 'better'; does society need people who have attained the kind of objectives that your course will have?

Aims and objectives

The questions in Figure 72, 'How shall I get there?' and 'How shall I know when I have arrived?' cannot be answered unless you know where it is you are going in the first place. Clarity about your aims and objectives is important. Unless you know where you are going, you are not likely to get there. Unless your pupils know what it is they are meant to learn, they are less likely to achieve whatever the purpose of your material was. Unless you know whether or not you have arrived at where you wanted to be, you cannot evaluate your progress in getting there or be in a position to know what changes or improvements to make.

Remember, though, that the journey there may be as important as the arrival, that your aim may be contained in the process rather than in the end product. For example, in fostering enquiry skills, the processes of finding a book by using the Dewey system, using an index, deciding what is relevant, taking notes, may be the real aim rather than the resulting essay.

What if the aims of the course are not being met?

Suppose, after evaluation, you find you are not meeting your objectives and not arriving at where you thought your course was taking your pupils? This raises other questions:

- *Are the objectives realistic?* Are you being too innovative for the teachers using the course, the pupils (and their parents) and the prevailing

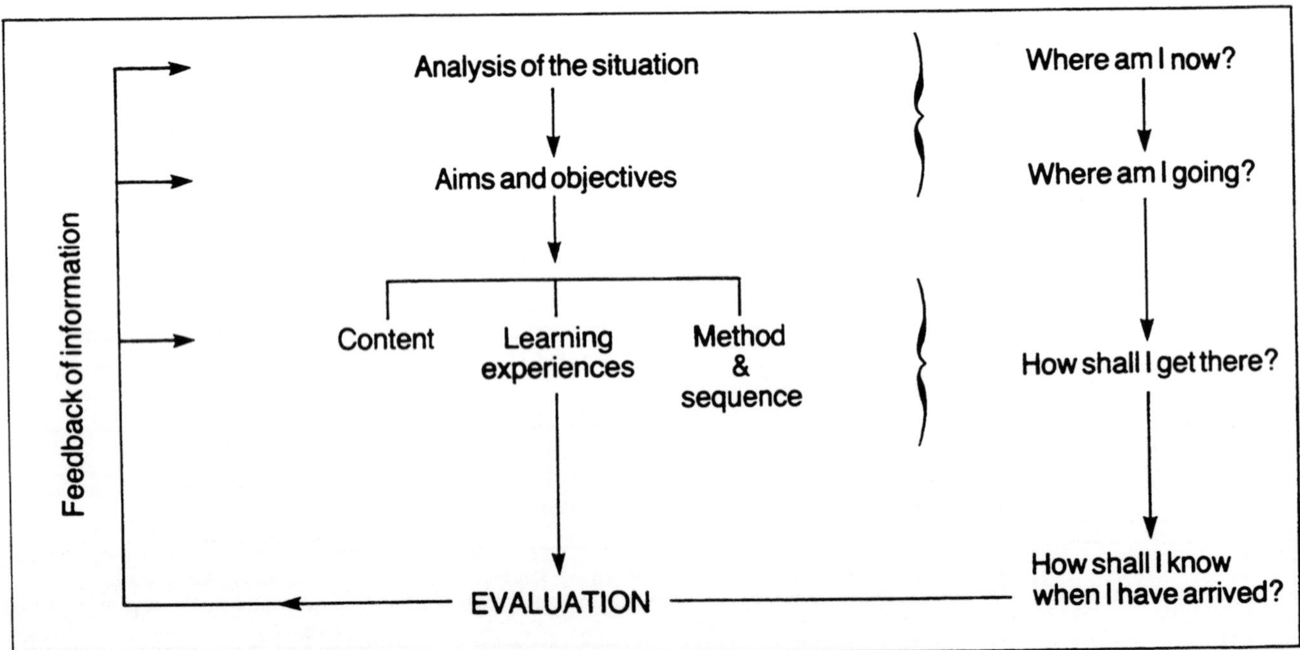

Figure 72 *Curriculum planning, including evaluation*

educational climate? Are you assuming background knowledge that the pupils didn't have? Are you expecting too much of them? Are you attempting too much in the time available?

- *Is there sufficient pupil motivation?* Perhaps pupils are not being given sufficient opportunity to gain a feeling of success and achievement. Is the course relevant to the needs of the pupils? Is it seen to be relevant? Perhaps more discussion of the aims and their relevance needs to be built into the course. Have changing job prospects lowered the level of motivation? In which case, perhaps you need to change the emphasis. Perhaps the pupils lack motivation because the material is plain dull. Is there enough variety in approach, in manner of presentation, in type of stimuli used? Are there incentives provided?
- *Are there unforeseen constraints and difficulties?* These might include absences; not as much time as you thought; a budget cut; staff shortages. If these are long-term, then you must reappraise your analysis of the situation and re-plan.
- *Are there deficiencies in your material or in your teaching methods?* If a large proportion of the pupils fail to meet the same objective or cannot answer the same test question, don't blame them - blame yourself and look for the cause. Have you pitched the material at too high a level? Is the language level appropriate? Are the learning steps too big? Are your wordings ambiguous, sentences too long? Are you using the right media for explaining your point? Are the pupils turned off because of poor visual quality? Is there sufficient explanation, guidance, support for the tasks you have set? Are you making sufficient allowance for the needs of the least able pupils in your class?

The answers to all these questions should provide feedback to the different stages in Figure 73 and provide information for decision-making about what changes are required. Always remember, even though all your aims have been met, if they are not worthwhile aims it is not a worthwhile course.

What other things can usefully be evaluated?

In addition to the effectiveness of your planned learning outcomes, there are other things to evaluate.

Were other, unplanned, outcomes revealed? All sorts of unexpected benefits occur. For example, you might have set up a group discussion to discuss some social issue. Your original aim might have been for the pupils to gain a better understanding of this issue. However, you find that what the pupils really get out of the situation is a greater tolerance for each other's points of view

PRACTICAL SKILLS DEVELOPED OR ATTEMPTED		UNIT 1	UNIT 2	UNIT 3
Construction/interpretation of tables of figures				
Construction/ interpretation of graphs	Block			
	Line			
Interpretation of cartoons				
Construction/interpretation of maps				
Construction/interpretation of pie charts				
Simulations/role playing				
Interpretation of data charts				
Construction/interpretation of diagrams				
Construction of surveys and questionnaires				
Interview skills				

Figure 73 *Checklist for a Social Studies course*

and a better group relationship. Don't waste this; include it in your aims and plan for it, so that it doesn't just happen by chance.

Often a teacher will modify, abandon or supplement his objectives according to the emerging needs or interests of his pupils. Sometimes there will be negotiation between teacher and pupils over objectives. An evaluation which was strictly in terms of the original objectives, and took no account of flexible situations such as these, could inhibit the evolution and growth of a course.

Keep a check on the time the course takes - some parts will take less time than you expected and some will take longer.

Is it time-effective? It may be a good course, but when you have reckoned up *your* time spent in preparation and organization, is it worth while? Moreover, is it cost-effective?

What variations were exhibited in the course? If

Comment arising from shredding session	Worksheet
Underline the word written 'triangle' (a point for the teacher to take up).	A triangle has 3 sides 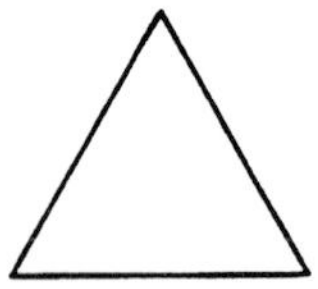
The word 'here' is misleading. There are 3 triangles at the bottom of the sheet, but there is another at the top. This is a problem of layout.	How many triangles can you see here?
The size and shape of the triangles could be more varied to emphasize that it is the 3-sidedness which defines a triangle.	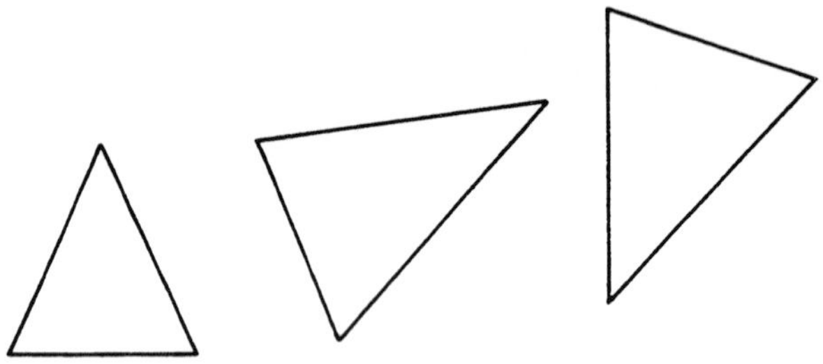

Figure 74 *Results of a shredding session!*

other teachers are using your material probably none used it in exactly the same way. Perhaps something can be learned from these variations.

With regard to classroom management, what problems and solutions emerged for the management of audio-visual aids and worksheets, or the arrangement of groups, outside visits etc?

If your course had aims for the development of the subject, new methodologies or media, have they succeeded or is the well-known phenomenon of 'innovation without change' taking place? (Teachers do the same old thing under a new name.) One of the severest tests of any new course is whether teachers do it again, and whether they carry on using it once the general support and emphasis surrounding a pilot project have been removed.

Some methods of evaluation for classroom use

Checklists

Lists are a useful way of checking whether your course has the required balance and variety, and whether all your stated objectives have been covered. The language matrix, discussed in Chapter 6 (Figure 34) is an example of such a checklist; Figure 73 is another.

Consulting colleagues

When you have written the first draft of your material, ask colleagues in your department to comment on it. If the material is designed for less able pupils or mixed-ability classes, also ask a Remedial Specialist to comment on it. Sometimes it is helpful if a person from another subject department looks at it – this gives a fresh angle nearer to the way the learner will see it.

Some people consider that the best evaluation is given anonymously – you are more likely to be told the truth. You may find this profoundly painful, but part of a teacher's professionalism is to accept useful criticism.

Two heads are better than one and discussions and 'shredding sessions' are invaluable at this stage – not only for correcting nitty-gritty details, but also for asking the big question. The author is nearly always too close to his own work to see the faults, or to see it in perspective.

Figure 74 is an example of the kinds of points the creator of the worksheet can so easily miss and which fresh eyes are more likely to see.

One-to-one

Select three pupils of known reading age and IQ from your class, one below average, one average and one above average. Sit down with each one in turn and go through the material, noting his or her reaction, which bits cause difficulty or misunderstanding, which bits take a long time and which bits are done quickly.

It is important that the pupils involved in an

Name John Smith

Date 11·6·76

Title Making an Electric Motor

Version Draft 2 (20·5·76)

Details of Student Age 16 Passed GCE 'O' level in Physics

Starting time: 10·15

Finishing time: 11·05

Frame Number	Comments	Proposed Action
2	✓	
3	✓	
4	looked back at frame 3	Ask student what problem was at end of session
6	✓	
7	✓ Took a long time	Check frame and ask student
9	X 'I don't understand the question'.	Modify ambiguous wording
10	X after adding an extra example to the frame, he got it right	Include this extra example in the frame
12	✓ performed practical exercise with considerable difficulty	Split frame into two parts
14	✓	
16	confused between millimetres and centimetres	Add introductory frame or pre-requisite test on metric units
18	x due to carelessness by student	No change

Figure 75 *Sample record sheet*

Source: 'Testing your Materials' by G. Manwaring & K. Menmuir, Learning Resources Unit, Dundee College of Education, 1978 evaluation of this kind understand that it is the material which is being tested and not themselves.

Figure 75 shows a record sheet used for evaluating a programmed text. A similar sheet could be used, substituting the frame numbers for page numbers, slide numbers etc.

Another way of closely monitoring pupils' reactions is to give them pens of two different colours (say blue and red) and ask them to underline in blue any section of the worksheet which they thought was really easy, and to mark in red the bits they thought were difficult or could not understand. The pooled results can provide useful feedback.

Classroom observation

There is no better way of finding out the strengths and weaknesses of a course than by teaching it. Only when the course is in action is learning taking place, and it is essential to evaluate your material not only on paper, but actually being used. Pupils will soon let you know which parts are interesting and motivating and which are not. However, you must keep a note of these observations. This might be in the shape of a record of work, a diary, or a special form for each unit or lesson. If more than one teacher is piloting the material, it helps to have everyone using the same system, so that notes are more easily compared and conclusions more easily drawn.

You may think that you can simply remember which bits went wrong and why; but you won't remember the all-important details, unless you write them down during or soon after the lesson.

Observation can also be used to evaluate classroom management. Did all those worksheets end up in a muddle? Was it really feasible to use an overhead projector, a tape recorder *and* a video machine? Were the seating arrangements appropriate to the occasion?

It can be very revealing to observe closely what pupils are actually doing in the classroom. Who are they talking to? What are they, in fact, talking about? What they are learning is not always what you imagine.

There follow three examples of different kinds of observation made in classrooms, each different in style of observation and evaluation from that suggested in the opening part of this section – your style of evaluation depends on the kind of evidence and information you are collecting and the type of decision or action you are intending to take.

1st Five Minutes

A B C

D E F

3rd Five Minutes

A B C

D E F

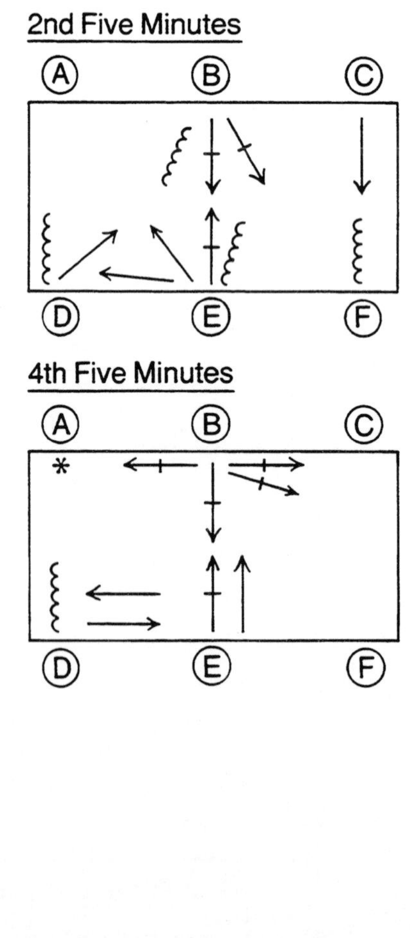

KEY

A	PUPIL
——→	TALK TO DO WITH WORK
—+→	TALK NOT TO DO WITH WORK
~~	LAUGHTER
*	QUESTION TO THE TEACHER
▭	WORK TABLE

Figure 76 *Example 20* (Examples 1 and 2 taken from *Curriculum in Action: An approach to Evaluation* Open University 1980).

Example 20
Classroom observations were carried out for four periods of five minutes (see Figure 76). A separate plan was used for each period. The group observed in detail was fairly typical of the rest in the class.

Notes made immediately after the lesson
When talking, pupils all continued working, except for **B** who stopped working when making a point.

D and **E** had a discussion about work that **D** was doing which involved **E** handling **D**'s work. (2nd five-minute period).

B appeared to be a conductor of most conversations. (What would have happened if **B** had not been present?)

A asked me a question, but did not communicate with the others at all, even when a question was directed at him. (4th five-minute period).

F did not talk to any of the group, but was listening and joining in with laughter.

Looking at their work, and assessing it, I would suggest that there may be a correlation between quality of work and amount of talking in this case. The work **B** produced was of poor quality, unimaginative. The work **A** produced was sensitive, skilful and well finished off.

I was surprised by the amount of laughter.

Much of the talk concerned music on the radio that was playing in the background. Is this a good or a bad thing?

The observation confirmed that **A** is an isolate. I was surprised at the amount of talk from **B**.

Example 21
13 February 1980
Third-year remedial science, 9.30 - 10.00 a.m.
Observation period - fifteen minutes in the middle of the lesson.

I have selected my Combined Science group as being the most useful and interesting for evaluation. This is a third-year remedial group who are taught as a form set and have been since they entered the school.

The remedial groups in this school tend to be very immature and to have a strong sense of their own failure. On the whole, the children are ashamed to be in the group and their learning seems to be inhibited merely by belonging to the group.

I feel disturbed about the feeling in the group and started the year determined that their work would be relevant to the children and their stage of development.

This has proved very difficult and, although I have abandoned the suggested syllabus, I have as yet not achieved cooperation or motivation for this group. I thought it might widen my understanding to attempt to answer the questions using this group.

I selected this period before the lesson began and deliberately planned a short period when I could take notes. This was not particularly easy as this group demands continuous attention. Because they tend to be very immature, petty arguments can result in physical disagreement which can be dangerous if allowed to develop in a laboratory.

During the term the children have been learning about very simple animals and plants (e.g. fungi and tapeworms) and I have selected examples which would be interesting for the children and give them a chance to relate anecdotal experience. In this lesson the concept of classification is to be introduced. Pictures of unidentified animals and plants have been placed round the room and after a short introduction the children are asked to look at the pictures, identify the animal or plant and try to place it in a group (e.g. mammal, reptile, moss etc.).

This was set in the form of a competition and therefore I could not offer too much assistance and was free to make limited notes.

Question 1: What did the children actually do?
They were sitting round my desk having various conversations. Gary and David turned the taps on slightly and used rulers to flick water at each other. Pauline was telling Jeanette about her bedroom, Angela and Carol quickly joined in. They do not appear to really listen to each other, but are very anxious to make their points. Eventually, they listened to a suggestion that they might be able to visit the museum and then listened to suggestions of a game to divide animals into groups. Most start to get up before they know what they really have to do and then return to their seats. They make loud bored noises when reminded of the work covered so far and ask questions about the museums in the area. When instructions are complete they rush to the nearest pictures. They seem interested and talk about the animals to each other. Mainly they try to convince each other that they are right. They are working in small groups which cooperate, but argue with any other group wanting the same pictures. Carol and Pauline are diverted by some apparatus on the window sill, but after a quick look return to the pictures. Gary is making silly noises and begins arguing with Russell over ownership of a pencil. Gary pushes Russell who gives back the pencil and goes back to the pictures. Children bring pictures or shout questions to me about the animals they are looking at.

All return to my desk with pictures (collected by Carol) for identification. Angela was still working when Carol collected the pictures and they shouted at each other, but without actual anger.

Question 2: What were they learning?
They cannot play a game without full instructions.

They must not play with taps. (This has already been learned, but reinforcement seems to have little effect.)

There are animals and plants they do not recognize, but they can put them in groups by looking for characteristics (e.g. hair, backbone, shell, etc.).

They learn to share knowledge with other members of the group.

Question 3: How worthwhile was it?
This was one of the most successful lessons I have spent with this group and I think it was worth while both in terms of learning about animal groups and their characteristics, and in sharing knowledge. This has not previously taken place, but on this occasion they all recognized some animals and could therefore contribute. Are my lessons usually too difficult?

Attendance is a problem in remedial groups and perhaps total lack of interest is partly due to lack of an overall picture of the course. Does this mean that every lesson for this group must be complete in itself? This would make it very difficult to build on existing knowledge.

Question 4: What did I do?
Before the lesson I spread cards with pictures of unidentified animals and plants around the room. I gained quiet and attention by mentioning the museum (we are going next month). I stopped Gary and David flicking water at each other. I gave instructions for playing the game.

Question 5: What did I learn?
I learned that it is possible to let this group work without me without serious fights developing. While planning this lesson I thought the game might be too simple, but apparently it was not and it gave some a much needed chance to share information with others.

I found that they are very interested in animals and know more than I expected about grouping them.

Question 6: What do I intend doing now?
As this has been one of my most successful lessons with this group, I shall attempt to use the experience. I shall carry on with the topic of classification, but at a simpler level than originally intended, and include tasks which allow the children to move about and to increase their knowledge without having to come to terms with language which is outside their experience. I should listen to them more often!

It will be both useful and interesting for me to continue making observations of this group throughout the course.

Example 22
Figures 77 and 78, pp. 108, 109 and 110, show records of two pupils' behaviour patterns, observed closely over fifteen and thirty minutes respectively.

Tests

The purpose of giving tests, in this instance, is to find out whether the objectives of your course are being met by a majority of the pupils.

If you are already using criterion-referenced assessment and diagnostic tests with your class, these will tell you all you need to know for the purpose of evaluating the material and the course. However, if tests are normally given only to establish a class order, you may have to give a different test.

For evaluation purposes you are not seeking to gain a spread of marks and to establish which pupil is better than the other, but to discover how many pupils have reached a predetermined standard for each objective.

A record of test results in tabular form (see Figure 79, p. 111) will show which items need to be overhauled. For diagnostic purposes, where the focus is on the pupil, you would look *across* the columns. You should see, for example, that James is having difficulty, having mastered only one of the five skills. For the purposes of evaluating the material, you would look *down* the columns. Now you see that all pupils have mastered the map symbols, but only one has mastered the concept of scale and more than half the group has difficulty with orientation. The materials and teaching methods used for scale and orientation obviously need to be reconsidered. Remember that not all learning objectives can be assessed by means of formal tests.

Asking the pupils
Asking pupils what they thought of the course can be useful – which parts did they like, which didn't they like, what improvements could they suggest? However, if you are making careful and accurate observation, during the pilot stage, most of these answers should be known to you. Reports have to be fairly detailed to be of much use and one-word or one-sentence answers aren't all that helpful. It is not always easy to create the openness and honesty necessary for accurate feedback from pupils, nor to overcome the tendency of some pupils to say what they think you want to hear.

A cautionary tale! In evaluating a course which involved pupils in going to a hospital for community work, I asked the pupils if they had enjoyed it: 'Great. We liked sitting in the back of the bus on the way there and smoking.' But what pupils say in front of each other out of bravado is not necessarily what they really think. Nearly all

RECORD OF ONE PUPIL'S BEHAVIOUR.

School 23RX ST. 28.11.1975

Pupil's Code Name - Scatterbrain

	UNPRODUCTIVE ACTIVITY		TEACHER CONTACT		WORKING	
	m	s	m	s	m	s
Playing, looking round, using pencil as gun	1	35				
Looking at teacher showing slides to girls	1	55				
Just looking round the class	1	15				
Starts to write (Why start now?)						
Looks atreference sheet						25
Writing in own folder						12
Gets up, goes to drawer - collects a						36
new sheet of paper and then starts to wander round class. Waits by teacher.	1	15				
Talks to teacher				5		
Returns to desk		10				
Is getting ready to work Uses rubber band as catapult Collects a pencil from box on other side of room, examines overhead projector	1	50				
Distracted by teacher		5				
Thinking about work then rules lines and draws in own folder						52
Stops work for a rest		2				
Starts work again and continues for a few seconds						5
Stops again - walks off, general tour of class	1	50				
Goes to teacher's desk Plays with rubber band as catapult out of sight of teacher then waits with hand in pockets		58				
Speaks to teacher				38		
Goes to another teacher on the instructions of first teacher		30				
Collects coin (to draw round) and				2		
returns to own desk. Wanders off for unknown purpose		15				
Returns and recommences work						7
Stands up, pirouettes to relieve tension and sits down again		9				
Class called to order by teacher						
	11	4		45	2	17

Later observed working for 15 minutes

Figure 77 *Example 22*

RECORD OF ONE PUPIL'S BEHAVIOUR.

SCHOOL: 23 RX ST. 28.11.1975.

Pupil's Code Name - requested observation.

Type of behaviour	Number of incidents	Time in seconds			Percentage
		Total	Average	Range	
A. RESEARCH ACTIVITY Reading source materials and associated worksheets.	4	274	68.5	5-235	15.4
B. OVERT PRODUCTIVE ACTIVITY Writing, drawing Occasional consultation* of source material (*Distinguished from A in that pen still poised ready to continue)	19	1265	66.6	7-224	71.1
C. SEEKING NEW MATERIAL OR EQUIPMENT Going to collect something	4	44	11.0	7-20	2.5
D. TEACHER CONTACT					
1. Waiting for teacher (Hand raised - looking for - queuing)	3	57	19.0	7-25	3.2
2. Interactions with teacher	3	39	13.0	11-13	2.2
E. PRIVATE ACTIVITY					
1. Thinking/Day dreaming	2	88	44.0	35-53	4.9
2. Talking/consulting with neighbour	1	12	12-	12-	0.7
F. OBSERVATION SUSPENDED. Observer unable to see or otherwise distracted	2	15	7.5	7-8	

Figure 78 *Example 22*

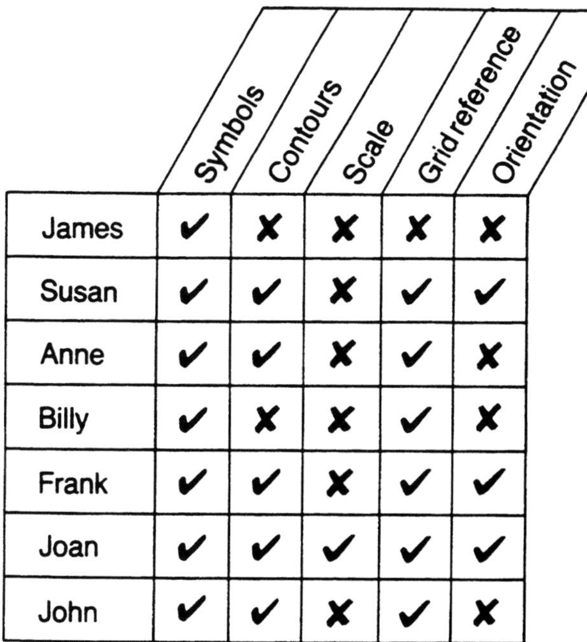

	Symbols	Contours	Scale	Grid reference	Orientation
James	✔	✘	✘	✘	✘
Susan	✔	✔	✘	✔	✔
Anne	✔	✔	✘	✔	✘
Billy	✔	✘	✘	✔	✘
Frank	✔	✔	✘	✔	✔
Joan	✔	✔	✔	✔	✔
John	✔	✔	✘	✔	✘

Figure 79 *Test results for first-year map reading unit*

those pupils went back to the hospital during the school holidays, paying their own travel, to continue helping voluntarily. That was a much truer indication of the success of the course. And similarly, a close watch on attendance patterns might indicate the popularity of a course better than what the pupils actually say. A more fruitful line of enquiry might be to ask pupils about their perception of the worth of the course. Do they place value on its aims? Is it relevant to their own perceived needs and view of themselves?

Teacher impression
Where other teachers are involved, their comments can be very useful. A fairly common procedure is to ask for written reports and then to arrange interviews with one or two of those teachers whose reports indicate that even more useful feedback might be obtained by following up their replies. It is sometimes useful if the teacher keeps a period by period log or diary of the trial course. Group discussions with all the teachers involved, and a final 'shredding session' before the final rewrite, can also be valuable.

Figure 80, overleaf, shows an example of an evaluation report form to bring all the feedback together.

Summary of evaluation methods

In Table 13 I summarize some of the chief advantages and disadvantages of various evaluation methods.

Table 13
A summary of some evaluation methods

Method	One advantage	One disadvantage
Group discussion	A number of views aired. These views have to be explained fully and justified.	Can be dominated by 'leaders' who may 'bend' the group feelings. Huge quantity of data much of which is lost. Wide-ranging.
In-depth interviews	Probe reasons for opinions. May reveal important rather than superficial points.	Easy to lose sight of evaluation purpose and become involved in peripheral problems.
Pre and Post-testing	Enables evaluator to assess the amount of learning progress. Gain score.	May divert attention from other effects of the course than the achievement of objectives.
Post-testing	Allows evaluator to assess the level to which the course objectives have been achieved.	Does not always indicate how much they have learnt from the course itself rather than from other sources.
Observation	Those observed may not know what you are looking for or even that they are being observed. Spontaneous. Probably closer to reality than other methods.	Frequently lacks precision. Interpretation difficult.
Developmental testing	Allows continuous refinement	Can interfere with the smooth running of the course.
Pilot teacher	In a position to spot particular difficulties – frequent contact with and observation of students. Participant observers. Can reach student problems and achievement. Aware of quality of products.	Can be delivered in a context of interstaff jealousies. May not be reliable.
A colleague's view	Friendly and frank view	You may like him because he agrees with you
Pupil views	They are the consumers, the only people who can give you a first hand response.	Pupils find it difficult to respond.

(i) *Teacher Information*

1. Please rate the following items on a five point scale by circling the appropriate number.

   1 = Very good/useful etc.
   5 = Very bad/useless etc.

   (a) Clarity of teacher's notes 1 2 3 4 5
   (b) Helpfulness of teacher's notes 1 2 3 4 5
   (c) Usefulness of statement of objectives 1 2 3 4 5
   (d) Usefulness of the suggested approach 1 2 3 4 5

2. Please write in your comments on the following topics:—

   (a) How far did you agree with the objectives of the unit?
   (b) Alternatives/additions to the 'suggested approach'
   (c) Provision of information on the content of the unit (i.e. information for the teacher)
   (d) General comments on teacher information

(ii) *Pupil Information*

1. Again rate the following items on a five point scale.

   1 = Very good
   5 = Very bad

   (a) Language used in information sheet(s) 1 2 3 4 5
   (b) Length of information sheets 1 2 3 4 5
   (c) Content of information sheet(s) 1 2 3 4 5
   (d) Presentation of information sheets 1 2 3 4 5

2. Please outline any general comments you have about the content, presentation etc. of pupil information.

Pupil Worksheets

1. Again rate the following topics on a five point scale.

   1 = Very good
   5 = Very bad

   (a) Language used in worksheet(s) 1 2 3 4 5
   (b) Length of worksheet(s) 1 2 3 4 5
   (c) Layout of worksheet(s) 1 2 3 4 5
   (d) Activities in worksheet(s) 1 2 3 4 5

2. Please add any general comments you have about the worksheets.

Audio-visual aids

Please list and comment on any of the following used with the unit.

(a) *Films*
(b) *Filmstrips*
(c) *Radiovision/tape-slide etc.*
(d) *Overhead Projector Transparencies*
(e) *Tapes*
(f) *Poster*
(g) *Other visuals or sound aids*

Miscellaneous

1. Please rate the following topics on a five point scale.

   1 = Very good/well etc.
   5 = Very bad/poorly etc.

   (a) Pupil interest 1 2 3 4 5
   (b) Length of whole unit 1 2 3 4 5
   (c) Educational value of whole unit 1 2 3 4 5
   (d) Degree to which objectives were met 1 2 3 4 5

2. Please add any general comments you have about unit as a whole.

Figure 80 *An evaluation report form* Source: University of Bristol, Dept. of Education.

Chapter Twelve

An invitation to the party

This chapter is aimed at teachers who are or are likely to become members of working parties producing material for people other than themselves. Skip this chapter if you do not recognize yourself in this description.

Producing materials for other users is a very different matter from producing it for your own use and raises a variety of questions and problems which do not occur when you are your own customer. There are different problems, too, when a group rather than an individual is involved. Different styles, assumptions and ways of working have to be welded together. As the scale of production of worksheets and allied resources increases, answers to questions about reprographics, packaging or cost-effectiveness may not be the same as the answers you would come up with if you were producing the unit for one class or one year group.

Since most working parties disband once their task is completed, the experience gained and the solutions found to these problems tend to be lost and rediscovered over and over. It is my hope that this chapter will capture and make available to you at least some of this ephemeral expertise.

Working parties and curriculum development

Working parties are usually set up to pioneer some new area of the curriculum, to respond to a need for change, or to support or implement innovations recommended by DES or local authority reports. In short, the majority of working parties are fulfilling a role as agents of change. You might find it worth while clarifying where you stand in relation to the following questions.

Which of these roles describes your working party?

- *Catalyst* – producing exemplar material; identifying and supporting 'front runners' or 'growth points'.
- *Solution giver* – working on particular problems identified by others; finding out what works and what doesn't; trying to apply recommendations in a practical classroom situation.
- *Resource provider* – producing 'package' courses etc. to support innovations which have already been worked out and accepted.

Which of the major strategies of innovation is your working party adopting?

- A *problem-solving* strategy. Here the starting point is an expressed need on the part of the user. The initiative comes from the user and the working party will be mainly comprised of the ultimate users of the material. Research indicates that self-initiated and self-applied innovation has the strongest user commitment and the best chance of long-term survival.
- The *'research development and diffusion'* strategy. Here the initiative comes from outside. A 'package' is developed and disseminated. The user is not generally involved in its production and is a passive recipient. There is an assumption that a rational consumer will adopt innovation if the reasons for doing so are sound enough.

What is the degree of innovation implied by the work of your group?

- *Marginal.* This adds to a teacher's repertoire rather than alters it.
- *Incremental.* This alters a teacher's style but not his role.
- *Fundamental.* This changes both style and role.

Do your aims tend towards the Utopian model or towards the deficiency model?
In the former, the goals set are optimistic and often imply major changes to behaviour and attitude – e.g. to bring about an ability to develop satisfactory personal relationships with others. The deficiency model takes a pessimistic view and makes assumptions such as: pupils lack motivation, are immature, come from 'unsatisfactory' family backgrounds.

Is your working party encouraging 'spectators' or 'players'?
Which of the following curriculum verbs would be most typical of your course?

Spectators	*Players*
acquire knowledge	act
describe	do
study	plan
explain	organize
understand	make
memorize	create

Is the material you are producing a starting point for development or an end point?
Are you aiming at a 'teacher-proof' package, or at

one in which the user is invited to take part, to make choices, to adapt, add or extend? If after five years no sign of the original material remains, i.e. it has been subject to a continuous process of growth and change, would you regard this as a sign of success or failure?

Are there barriers to your material being accepted by other people?
Is the innovation too big a step for teachers to feel comfortable with? Is the material too complex? Does it present too many classroom management problems, or require too much preparation? Is it too daunting? Does it require too many extra resources, and is it too expensive? Is in-service training required by the users?

It may just suffer from the NIH factor (Not Invented Here). People prefer something they have been involved in from the start.

Remember, curriculum design does not become curriculum development until it is actually implemented in the classroom and continues after the extra support, which is often associated with pilot projects, has been withdrawn.

Is your group clear about its developmental objectives?
We tend to think of objectives in terms of the learning outcomes for the pupils, but a course can also have developmental objectives aimed at the teacher. These should be clearly stated. Examples 23 and 24 will give you some ideas.

Example 23

Course aims for the teacher

- to provide a common course in Modern Studies within the division and, through such a course, to establish common ground for discussion, in-service training and resource provision and sharing;
- to act as an exemplar to teachers of approaches to mixed-ability teaching using criterion-referenced and diagnostic testing;
- to provide a total package, with in-built assessment systems to aid (a) teachers who are new to the subject or may not have taught it in S1/S2 before; (b) teachers who have not previously prepared material, using the core and extension approach and using criterion-referenced tests.

Example 24

Targets
As visual literacy and study of the film media are areas of the curriculum which barely receive recognition in some schools, there is room for further exploration and development in this field. It is hoped that the packaged course 'Understanding Picture and Sound' will make some contribution in this direction, but, by itself, it would represent only a very small proportion of the total school curriculum. Therefore, it is important to ask what happens after this particular course has come to an end. If visual literacy is to expand and develop in schools it is not enough just to make use of this package; both its authors and its users must set targets outside its immediate boundaries. Such targets must be concerned both with the development of the curriculum and with the professional development of individual teachers. Some suggested targets are presented here as a basis for discussion.

One or more years after using this package you will be able to respond positively to the following questions:

- Are you continuing to concern yourself with visual literacy as a worthwhile part of the curriculum?
- Have you extended, developed or adapted any of the approaches suggested in the package? To what extent have you used the package as a starting point for further development?
- Have you formed links with other teachers in extending these ideas – particularly teachers of English, Art, Music, Speech and Drama?
- Through in-service training, the suggested reading and your own researches, have your own understanding and appreciation of visual literacy increased?
- Has your use of non-verbal means of expression increased in other areas of your teaching? Do you employ any of the following approaches to a greater extent than before:
  Concepts of iconography and genre
  Planning and editing in picture and sound
  Use of tape/slide and cine film
  Use of animation techniques
  Study and analysis of film
  Greater use of audio-visual aids in general
- Has anything you have done or said encouraged other teachers to try these approaches?

No doubt you can add several aims of your own and it is hoped that this package will provide some measure of support in implementing them.

What format are you using?

Table 14 shows categories of material in terms of the degree of structure involved. Freedom, flexibility and teacher autonomy of unstructured materials must be weighed against the much greater degree of guidance, preparation and support provided for the teacher by structured materials. Your decision may depend on who is

Table 14

Category	*Format*
Resource box	Unstructured resources and teacher information
Resources and suggestions	Minimal structure
Resources and related activities and worksheets	Semi-structure
Individualized learning materials	Highly structured e.g. a programmed learning unit

likely to use the material and on how you see the role of other potential users of your material.

Another decision concerning format is whether or not your worksheets are expendable. Do you word instructions so that pupils respond in their jotters/notebooks or on the actual sheet?

The whole question of reprographics and distribution needs to be thought out. If the policy is to distribute single copies only to each school so that they can photocopy the required number, then it might be better to issue the material in ring-binders rather than in stapled booklets which would have to be dismantled. If schools rely mainly on Banda machines, then it might be more appropriate to issue the course in the form of Banda masters.

Adequate provision for other users

There is a big difference between producing material for your own use and producing material for use by other teachers. There are many things which you, the author, understand, assume, keep in your head etc. which must be spelled out in detail, on paper, for other users. An introduction or Teacher's Guide/Handbook to the unit could usefully contain the following:

- who *exactly* the course is intended for;
- the rationale of the course;
- an indication of how the unit fits into the course as a whole;
- the aims and objectives for the pupils;
- the development aims for the teachers – e.g. the developments or innovations which this material will help the teacher to bring about; the new methods it will facilitate; if it is exemplar material, what it is an example of;
- an overview, general outline, or planning grid for the whole course, linking content, skills, vocabulary, resources, activities, assessment;
- a suggested procedure for working through the unit (indicating any alternative routes) – but beware of telling teachers their own business;
- a summary of the pilot phase – experience gained; pitfalls to be avoided; helpful suggestions arising from the pilot; an indication of time taken;
- a pre-planner – what needs to be done *before* the course starts, e.g. films to order, visits to arrange, resources to find, experiments to set up;
- discussion and guidelines concerning the approach to assessment;
- a checklist of resources included in the course;
- the script or a summary of any tapes or videos;
- any special note or warnings about safety hazards and precautions.

Working in a team

Method of working

Experience has shown that when a group gathers the most useful things to do are planning, coordination of activities, 'shredding', discussion of problems. The actual writing and production of material is better divided up and done by individuals or pairs. Less is done in two half days than in one whole-day meeting.

The ideal is a residential situation of two or three days, with facilities for the group to come together when needed or divide into smaller groups when appropriate. This kind of situation also enables the members to get to know each other. Until members of a group feel they know each other well enough to give and take criticism and can say to each other 'I think that is a load of rubbish' without causing offence, progress will be slow. Every group needs a convenor/chairman/coordinator and an overall editor.

The role of the chairman

Obviously the role will vary from one group to another according to the nature of the work, the composition of the group, and the general context in which the group is operating. In general, the chairman should maintain unity of purpose and approach whilst encouraging variety and allowing freedom to the enthusiasms of the individuals within the group. The chairman should have an overview and be aware of the wider context and implications.

Here are some fairly typical tasks of a working-party chairman:

- One of the most important tasks of the chairman is to maintain the morale and enthusiasm of the group. A final end-product two years away is too distant a goal. Try to arrange a series of attainable, short-term goals, with tangible, practical results so that the group can actually see that it has achieved something worth while.

- Be aware of what else is going on in the same field. This can save work, provide new ideas and perspectives and open up opportunities for liaison or dialogue with similar projects.
- Make sure that all members of the group understand the remit of the group, the exact extent and limits of the task in hand and the amount of work likely to be involved.
- Make sure that everyone understands and agrees on the aims and rationale of the course and the educational theories and assumptions behind these. In this way, any fundamental disagreements are less likely to emerge half way through the life of the group.
- Make sure that the basic parameters of the course are understood and agreed on – the target population, the length of the course, the money/resources available for the course, the method of assessment; whether 'core and extension' is to be used and if so, what goes into the core and what into the extension.
- Not all members of the team will be starting from the same level of skills, commitment or familiarity with the methodology involved. Where necessary, the chairman should distribute background information and examples of similar projects, relevant reports, 'starter' papers, arrange in-service training etc.
- Arrange division of tasks, schedules and deadlines and make sure that everyone keeps to them; make sure that procedures for evaluation of the course have been understood and are carried out; arrange meetings.
- Keep a minute of decisions made at meetings; make sure that all changes and modifications are noted on the 'master copy' of the draft; make sure that each draft or version is dated – it is all too easy to mix up different drafts and generally get in a muddle about what changes were or were not decided on.
- Maintain an overview of what is going on in the group and its different sub-groups. Ensure that there is good communication within the group and that everyone knows what is happening and has an overall picture.
- Liaise with the wider production team – the graphics designer, the audio-visual technician, the reprographics department, the typists and office staff. These people have a point of view too and usually appreciate being consulted rather than told; they also appreciate knowing how their work fits into the overall scheme. The chairman should have an awareness of what is possible technically and what is not – whether back to back printing is possible, whether photographs can be copied, whether a word processor is to be used or not etc. – these things will influence the options open to the writing team.
- Ensure that policies are agreed on about back-up resources. For example, if a course makes use of a film, how many films are purchased – one for each school, several held centrally? The same applies with sets of slides etc.
- What policy is best adopted for updating the course – periodic revision, replacement of used components?
- Produce a teachers' handbook/guide. This is the concern of all members of the group, but unless it is delegated as a particular responsibility it is likely to remain undone. The chairman or the editor is in the best position to 'pull it all together' and present the overview to the potential user.

The role of the editor

Editorial policy
If editorial policy is known from the start, much time can be saved. Figure 81 is an example of an editor setting out his policy to contributors in advance of their contributions.

Unity of structure. Policies required for editing a unit, or a series of units, of teaching material are not quite the same as those needed for individual articles. There must be an overall pattern and structure. For example, in a course which deals with certain issues at local, national and international level, each issue should be dealt with in the same order. It would confuse the pupil if one unit started with an international example and another unit with an example at local level. Similarly the general format should be the same throughout. If colour coding is used – white for teacher information, blue for core material, pink for extension material – obviously each unit must adopt the same colour code. It is not unusual to find that some units, but not others, have started with a statement of objectives and those that have are of different degrees of detail.

Unity of layout. Paragraphs should be numbered in the same way in each unit and guidelines given on when to use each system – decimal numbers, bracketed Roman numerals, alphabetical system etc. Similarly with tables, figures, diagrams. Systems of labelling and numbering can become incredibly complicated and confused.

There should be uniform systems for headings and sub-headings. There should be a uniform policy on the use of capital letters – are they used for

Notes for the guidance of contributors

TYPESCRIPTS should be typed double-spaced, on one side of the page, with indentation indicating new paragraphs. There should be no space between paragraphs, and pages should be numbered. Please do not staple the pages together — use a paper clip.

HEADINGS AND SUBHEADINGS should be in upper and lower case. (Remember that underlining indicates that he printer should set in italics.) There should be one line of space above but not below subheadings.

AUTHOR'S NAME should be at the beginning of the article in upper and lower case, without qualifications or decorations, follwed by a sentence giving relevant details of the author's present post/qualifications/experience.

ABSTRACT: the article should be headed by a brief abstract not more than ten lines long.

REFERENCES should appear at the end of the article in alphabetical order of authors.
References to books, eg:
MEDAWAR, P B, *The art of the soluble-creativity and originality in science,* Penguin, London, 1969
References to articles, eg:
DAVIES, E R, 'The role of self-paced study', *British Journal of Educational Technology,* 7, 3, 1976

ILLUSTRATIONS: figures, tables, etc, should be presented on separate sheets of paper, complete with captions, at the end of the typescript. The whereabouts of each illustration should be indicated in the text ('Table 1 about here'). Finished artwork for the lines should be provided when possible, though not necessarily for the lettering. Please note that half-tone illustrations (photographs) should be black and white, and of high quality.

FOOTNOTES: there should be *no* footnotes. Information should be either incorporated in the main text or given in notes at the end of the article.

QUOTATIONS: single inverted commas should be used throughout, except where double inverted commas are needed to indicate a quotation within a quotation. Quotations of more than five lines should have 2 line of space above and below.

SPELLING: in general please follow the Oxford English Dictionary: eg, -ize, -ization; judgement; inquire; focused; biased; cooperate.

ABBREVIATIONS: no full points — ie; eg; cf; etc; 5ft 2in; 3m; 13cm; 24gm; 80 per cent; USA; Dr; and so on.

DATES: 1 May 1983; 1960s; twentieth century.

NUMBERS: 310–11; 300,000. Numbers below ten should be written in full, and numbers above in written figures (eg, eight 80).

Figure 81 *'House Rules' issued by the Council for Educational Technology to those preparing text for the British Journal of Educational Technology* instructions only; for highlighting difficult words, or words which will be found in a 'word bank'; for emphasizing important points? If capital letters are used for more than one function, there is confusion.

Preferably one person should do all the drawings, so that they are in the same style. Failing that, there should be some coordination between the different artists.

Glossary. Do you have one or not? What words are included? Is there one big glossary at the end of the course or smaller ones with each unit?

Appendices. Do you need appendices? What goes into the body of the text and what is more appropriate in an appendix?

Cross-references. Do the writers refer to other chapters/units/sections, or is each part self-contained?

Bibliographies. Are these needed? Are they annotated? What is the style of setting them out?

Policy regarding obsolescence of information. In making out lists of useful addresses etc., it is better to give the title of a post, rather than the name of the person currently holding that position – e.g. 'The Secretary, The British Bear-Lovers' League', not 'Mrs. Todwell . . .'. In choosing examples, it is better to choose happenings that illustrate permanent issues, rather than being merely topical. These things are policy decisions and must be clearly laid down (after discussion).

This list is not exhaustive, but merely an indication of the kind of things that an editor needs to make policy decisions about for the guidance of the team *before* they start writing.

Editing for tone of voice and degree of formality

Some writers will adopt a formal, impersonal style, others will use a relaxed, informal, jokey style. Some will use the first person active voice, others will use the third person passive voice (see Figure 82). It is part of the editor's duty to impose a uniform 'tone of voice' on the material.

PASSIVE	The class were then given a test by the teacher	↑ Increasing formality
	The class were then tested by me	
ACTIVE	The teacher then gave the class a test	
	Then I gave 3c a test	

Figure 82 *Increasing formality of approach*

Strict paragraph numbering also tends to increase formality. This may be what you want. But if you want your text to be less formal, try to link the paragraphs in a more flowing and easy manner, without the use of numbers.

The way in which instructions are given or statements made sets the tone to a great extent:

'Teachers must use boxes round their diagrams.'

'You might find it helps improve both the look and the effectiveness of your diagrams if you put a box around them.'

The use of jargon is also a matter for the editor's judgement. It depends on who the target audience is. On the whole teachers are suspicious of jargon, but they are also professional people and if a generally accepted technical word can be used in place of ten non-technical words, there seems a case for using it.

Editing for detail

In the final editing, the editor needs to go through the text, carefully checking for any possible errors – errors of fact that have somehow slipped through the net, typing errors, minor inaccuracies such as 'McMillan' on one page and 'MacMillan' on another page. Attention to detail is important. Small mistakes can destroy the credibility of the material.

A common error to look out for is changes in the page numbering. The text might say 'see the example on page 10' whereas, owing to deletions, additions, altered layout etc., it has now moved to page 12. Similarly diagrams and tables have a habit of changing labels from one draft to another, – the text says 'see Table I' but the thing referred to is now labelled 'Diagram A'.

Headings and titles can vary from one member of the writing team to another. In a course I was helping to edit, some members had called it 'Cooperation and Conflict' and others had called it 'Conflict and Cooperation'. The words unit/module/sub-unit seemed to be interchangeable and there was no standard terminology on worksheet headings, the words 'remedial', 'revision' and 'extension I' all meaning the same thing.

Watch out for ambiguity: 'Take out pin, if bent, replace'.

Although a close scrutiny of language and vocabulary should be an important part of the evaluation process, the editor should also make a final check on language level and suitable choice of vocabulary for less able pupils.

Example 26

This example is of an article sub-edited for a newspaper. It is taken from *Editing and Design* by Harold Evans (Heinemann 1972). The original 'copy' is given first, and then the final article, simplified and shortened from the original:

> Uncertainty about mortgage rates has, in the last three months, limited the marked home-ownership advance of recent years, according to the National Federation of Building Trades Employers.
>
> A survey just completed shows that private house-purchase figures have fallen away sharply compared with three months ago.
>
> Despite the improvement in the availability of mortgages, the number of empty houses awaiting buyers is rising. A spokesman for the Federation yesterday blamed the situation on the Government's failure to say when, if and by how much, interest rates will be reduced.

- Fewer people are buying houses - because of uncertainty about mortgage rates, says the National Federation of Building Trades Employers.

  It is easier to get mortgages, but a Federation survey reveals more empty houses and fewer private purchases in the last three months. A federation spokesman yesterday blamed the Government for failing to say when, if and by how much interest rates will be cut.

Chapter Thirteen

In case you want some more

Although these examples and case studies are drawn from different subjects, they illustrate general principles and general do's and don'ts about writing worksheets. Please try to resist the temptation to look only at examples from your own subject or to skip this chapter altogether if your subject isn't here.

Case study 16

The worksheet in Figure 83 was written by a young teacher for a mixed-ability class of 13-year-olds in a comprehensive school. This was not a Geography lesson, but an introduction to a General Social Studies unit on Russia which dealt with such topics as Russia as a superpower, the political system in Russia, the education system, the economy etc. In its original form it was handwritten. The teacher was aware that there was room for improvement and asked me for advice. Prior to the worksheet being issued there had been no lead lesson. The comments following the example summarize the discussion I had with her, but were based on a much wider sample than the one worksheet presented here.

General comments (also see Table 15)

Worksheets should be typed. (Ask your school office or use the typewriter in the teachers' centre.)

The sheets look dull and uninteresting. The large blocks of type need to be broken up with pictures and maps.

Too great a proportion of the tasks set consist of 'write the answer in sentences'. A greater *variety* of activity is needed.

Too many tasks are simply transferring the facts from the information sheet to the jotter. Learning takes place more effectively if you can structure your questions so that your pupils have to *apply, interpret* or *process* the information in some way.

I don't think sufficient account is taken of the fact that this is for a mixed-ability class and some pupils are going to find the questions too difficult. Have you discussed your worksheets with the Remedial Specialist in your school?

Specific comments (also see Table 15)

This worksheet would have been a more fruitful learning experience if it had been the follow-up to a lead-lesson in which you had shown introductory slides/film of Russia and worked with the pupils in using an atlas.

Since this is the first worksheet of the unit how about telling your pupils what the unit is about? And why not tell them what they are supposed to learn by doing this unit! You could even be specific and say what they should know at the end of this worksheet. (What Ausubel calls 'advanced organizers'.) It stands to reason that your pupils are more likely to learn something if they know what it is they are supposed to be learning. Also it helps to make them partners in the learning process, rather than the worksheet being something done *to them* by the teacher.

I thought the worksheet was a little too impersonal for the average age of your class. Your starting point should have been your pupils, e.g. more comparison with their own country. How many of your pupils, I wonder, could point and show in which direction Russia is from where they sit in your classroom?

Much of the information could have been found out by the pupils for themselves from a good atlas. Your worksheet might have encouraged them to do this rather than telling them the facts.

Much of the information could have been presented visually through maps and diagrams. Your map is misleading – it looks like an island. What is land and what is sea? Since you neither provide a scale nor put the area shown in a wider context, it does not illustrate the point about size. All maps should have a scale, a compass, some indication of sea and land, a box to show where it begins and ends, and some heading.

Table 15

Teachers' questions	*Advisers's comment on specific questions*
1. How much of the world's land area is covered by the USSR? 2. How many times larger than Britain is the USSR?	This would be a much more meaningful activity if done visually. e.g. use graph paper and colour in the proportion of land that is the USSR.
3. How many time zones are there in the USSR?	The purpose of this unit is to convey the size of Russia – on which case the time *difference* is more relevant.
4. State the present population of the USSR.	This could be rather meaningless unless compared with the population of the UK. Again, this could be done visually/diagrammatically.

RUSSIA - SIZE AND POPULATION

The Union of Soviet Socialist Republics is the full name of one of the world's giant powers or SUPERPOWERS. The Soviet Union is the largest country in the world covering one sixth of the earth's surface.

Can you imagine a country twice the size of China, three times the size of the United States, ninety times the size of the United Kingdom? It spreads for 6000 miles across two continents - Europe and Asia - and through eleven time zones. That means that when a train starts its journey in Moscow on the 3000 mile trans-Siberian railway at 10.00 a.m., it is already 8.00 p.m. in Vladivostok at the other end of the line.

And what about the people who live in this vast country? Well there are about 268 000 000 of them for a start and they speak over 130 languages - although not all at the same time. The main language spoken in Russian, since as the table shows, over half of the population of the USSR are Russians.

National Group	Population (in millions)
Russian	135
Ukranian	44
Uzbek	11
Tartar	8
Armenian	6
Kazakh	7
Jew	3
Others	50

Figure 83 *Case study 16*

5. How many languages are there in the USSR? Which of these languages is the national language?	This bit could be enlivened and even made fun! e.g. copying the Russian alphabet, trying to write your name in Russian letters. Any possibility that your Modern Languages teacher might have a tape of the language being spoken?
6. Draw a bar chart to show the relative sizes of the different ethnic groups in the USSR.	I like the idea of asking them to translate the information from one form to another. This means they have to think about it. Will they understand the words 'relative' and 'ethnic'? Could your pupils possibly be directed to a picture of at least one of these groups in national dress?

Case study 17

The worksheet on the following two pages (Figure 84) was part of a Mathematics course for less able 15-year-old pupils.

The teacher has tried to make the exercise relevant to everyday life, interesting and visually appealing. Imagine the difference between this and the pages of printed problems which used to appear in the old style arithmetic books.

However, because of their small size of print, newspaper cuttings should be used with caution with less able pupils. Exercise 4 might present problems to some, and in exercise 5, the phrase 'according to official consumption figures' might cause a few head scratchings.

Case study 18

The effectiveness of humour and entertainment as teaching aids speak for themselves here. Notice how, in counting the syllables in 'motor', the rhyme of the next line helps the pupil check the answer. The shorter length of line compared with a prose passage also makes it easier for the eye to follow and more pleasing to look at on the page. My thanks are due to Jim McIntosh of the English Department of Dundee College of Education, whose verse this is.

Silly Bill

Words are funny and make me wonder
Where they come from (words like "blunder")
Words are made from little bits . . .
We call these "syllables",
Use your wits
To keep this long word in your head,
This strange word "syllables"
(You've just said).

Here's a word of syllables three,
(Count them!): "lollipop"
Do you agree?

Here's a word of syllables two,
(Count them!): "Wiz-ard",
Will that do?

Now here's more, are you ready, yet?
How many syllables do you get?
"Car" has . . .
And "motor" has . . .
Here's a difficult one for you:
"Dinosaur" and "dragonfly",
Count the syllables, go on, try
This might beat you, ask your teacher.
If you're puzzled, he's (she's) a clever creature:
"Detrimental", "conflagration",
Count the bits in "railway station".

Just to finish, do your best
To count all the syllables, east to west.
In a line of verse, all strung together,
Easy as lifting a feathery feather.

Here's the line, get steady, count,
See if you get the right amount:
"I like words, they're really queer"
(Did you count, how many
Write the answer here:)

I hope your head
Forever will be fillable,
With lots of words
As nice as SYLLABLE.

Case study 19

Worksheets are often thought of as being connected only with written responses. Figure 85 (p. 123) shows otherwise.

Case study 20

This example (Figures 86(a) and (b), p. 126) is taken from a course on 'Communications' for 13-year-old pupils, produced at the Multi-Media Resource Centre, Kennoway, Fife, Scotland.

The example compares the first draft of a worksheet (a) with the final version (b). To reach the final version the worksheet went through three different drafts, being commented on and shredded by the production team, with the editor collating their comments and making the final decisions. The main changes along the way from (a) to (b) were:

- title of unit 'Transport 2' inserted and worksheet heading changed to 'The 24-Hour Clock' (thought to be more descriptive of content than 'Mind How You Go 7');
- sub-headings '12-Hour System', '24-Hour Clock System' and columns used instead of the more awkward 'is written in a timetable as'.

The two examples and exercises are put side-by-side. The reference to a model 24-hour clock is cut

CHANGING SPEEDS

The graph below can be used to change a speed in miles per hour into a speed in kilometres per hour.

EXAMPLE A queenfish can swim at a speed of 50 mph.

Change this speed into km/h.

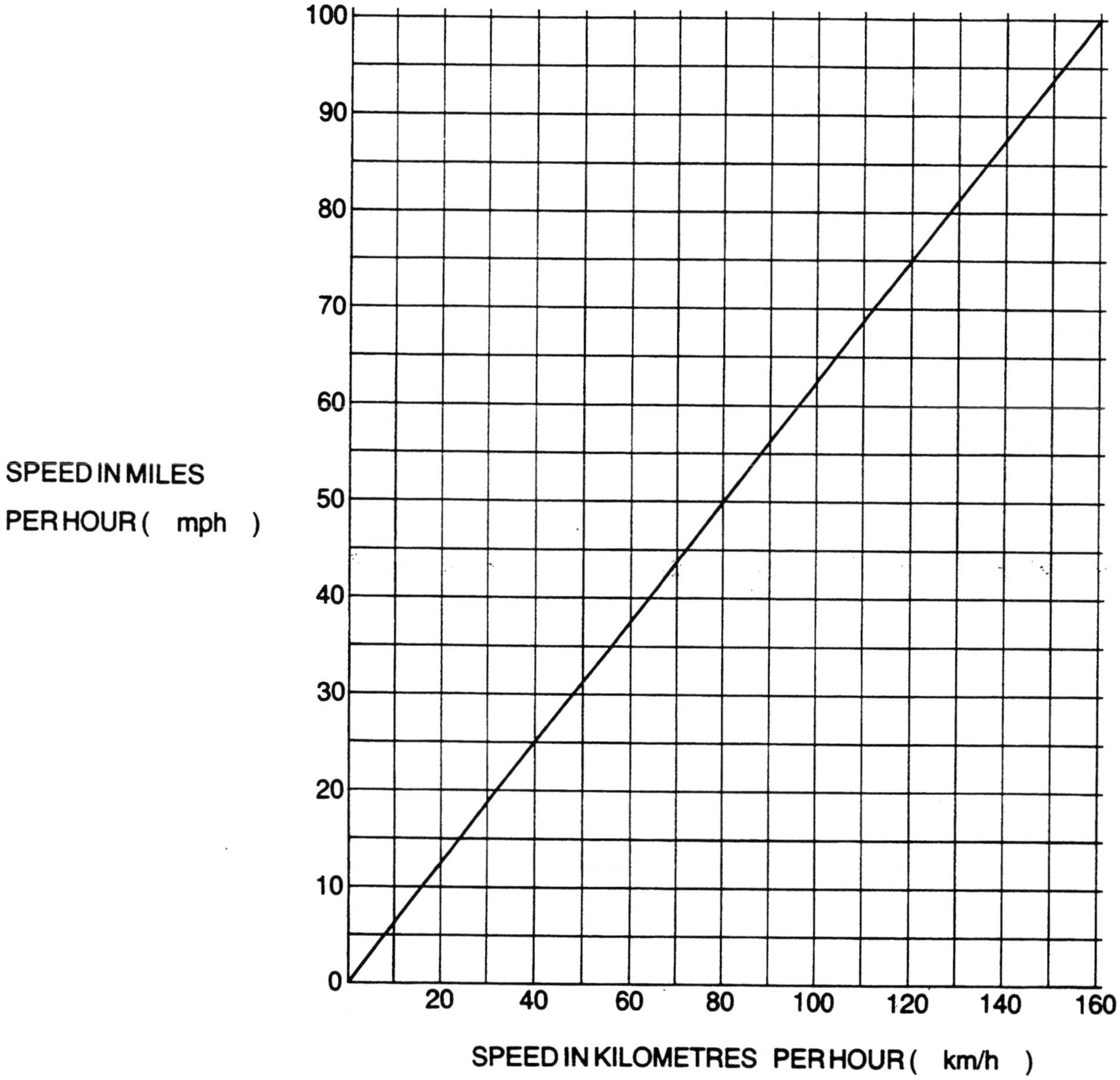

Vertical axis	SPEED IN MILES PER HOUR (mph) — 0, 10, 20, 30, 40, 50, 60, 70, 80, 90, 100
Horizontal axis	SPEED IN KILOMETRES PER HOUR (km/h) — 20, 40, 60, 80, 100, 120, 140, 160

ANSWER A queenfish can swim at a speed of 80 km/h.

Figure 84(a) *Case study 17*

Exercise (Use the GRAPH to answer these questions.)

(1)

THE TRAIN driver at the centre of the BR fiddle row told an inquiry yesterday that he drove a packed commuter train at more than 100 miles an hour.

Change the speed into km/h and rewrite the sentence about the train driver.

Driven back to speed traps

By DAVID STOAKES

A POLICE force which decided to trust motorists and scrap radar traps is bringing them back because of a rise in speeding offences.

In Britain these road signs tell us the speed limits in mph.

Change the speed limits into km/h.

(3)

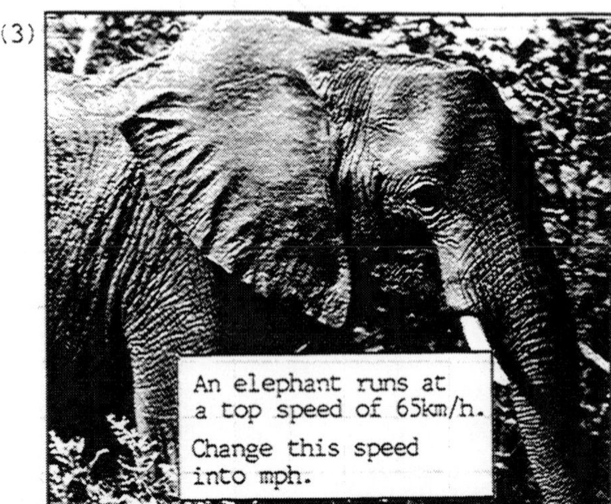

An elephant runs at a top speed of 65km/h.
Change this speed into mph.

(4)

"As you go down the in-run (just before take-off), you're just sensing the conditions of the snow with your feet finding a rhythm."

A rhythm: The jumper has fractionally over four seconds from the moment he launches himself down the precipice to the point at which he hits the lip at 60 miles an hour . . . and becomes airborne.

Travelling at some 80 feet per second, he has barely a tenth of a second to time his downward thrust for the lift-off.

Change the speed in miles an hour into km/h.

What could the speed in feet per second be changed into?

(5)

GTE
Acceleration from 0 to 60 m.p.h. takes 10.3 seconds, yet it is capable of up to 37.7 miles to the gallon according to official consumption figures.

Change the speed into km/h. and rewrite the sentence.

Figure 84(b) *Case study 17*

YOUR CHEST

- Cut out the pieces drawn below
- Arrange them correctly, then glue them into your book
- You may like to colour in the different parts

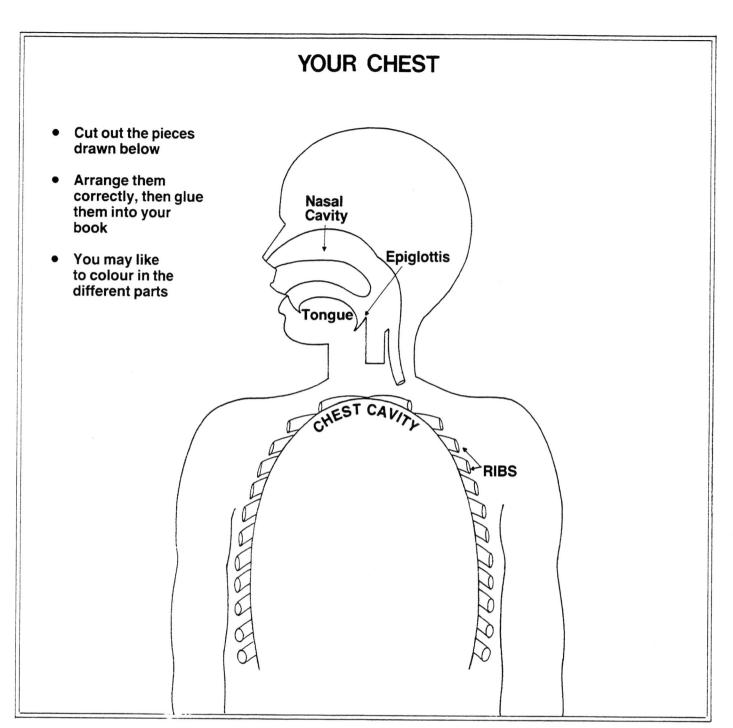

Nasal Cavity

Epiglottis

Tongue

CHEST CAVITY

RIBS

SPECIAL INSTRUCTIONS

- Do not glue down this side of the dotted line.
- Underneath this part of the lung place the heart, so that about $\frac{1}{3}$rd of it is covered by the lung.
- Reminder – the left lung is on the right as you look at the body

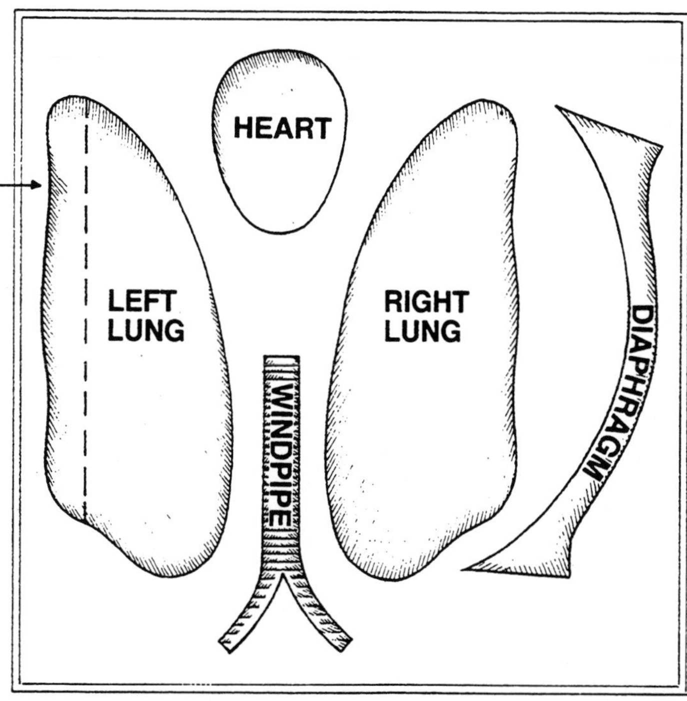

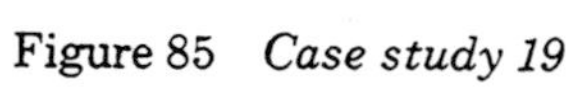

Figure 85 *Case study 19*

out (the model was going to be too costly and created organizational problems). In its place is the sentence 'Obtain Information 2 and use it to help you to convert the times given below.'

The worksheet is made more personal and less theoretical by introducing Henry Simpson and his holiday to Spain. A visual example using a wrist-watch is added. (In a previous draft a clock was used, but this was thought to be less personal than a watch.)

~~Often~~ Most timetables which have to do with transport use the 24 hour clock system.

Obtain the model 24 hour clock and use this to convert the times below.

Example 9.20 am. is written in a timetable as 09.20 hours.

~~10.45~~ 7.30 a.m. " " " " " " ______ hours

~~11.23 a.m.~~ 4.15 pm " " " " " " ______ hours

~~3.45~~ 9.45 p.m. " " " " " " ______ hours

12.00 noon " " " " " " ______ hours

12.00 midday " " " " " " ______ hours

Example 09.20 hours would read ~~11.40 hours~~ on your watch as 9.20 a.m.

05.30 hours ~~12.30 hours~~ ______

11.15 hours ~~15.40 hours~~ ______

01.45 hours ~~19.05 hours~~ ______

15.30 hours ______

22.15 hours ______

If Fred Bloggs starts a journey at 06.40 hours and finishes it at 15.20 hours, how long does the journey take? . . . .

The 24 hour clock system makes this sort of calculation easier.

You must also be able to convert times given on the 24 hour clock system into the 12 hour system which uses before midday (a.m.) and after mid-day (P.M.)

Figure 86(a) *Case study 20*

Most transport timetables use the 24 Hour Clock System. You must, therefore, be able to convert times given in the 12 Hour System into the 24 Hour Clock System, and vice versa.

Obtain Information 2 and use it to help you to convert the times given below. The first example of each type has been done for you.

12 Hour System		24 Hour Clock System
9.20 am	-	09.20 hours
7.30 am	-	
4.15 pm	-	
9.45 pm	-	
12.00 noon	-	
12.00 midnight	-	

24 Hour Clock System		12 Hour System
09.20 hours	-	9.20 am
05.30 hours	-	
11.15 hours	-	
01.45 hours	-	
15.30 hours	-	
22.15 hours	-	

Henry Simpson, who lives in Leven, Fife, is taking his family on holiday to Benidorm in Spain. In the table below you will see the times on Henry's watch at the various stages of the journey.

Figure 86(b) *Case study 20*

Appendix I

Check list

The questions listed here would not all apply to every worksheet, but would apply to the worksheets of a course or unit taken as a whole.

Are your worksheets/do they:

Planning and overview

- part of a planned, balanced and coherent course?
- pursue worthwhile aims and criteria?
- tell the pupils what these aims are?
- attempt a full range of skills and not over-emphasize knowledge and recall of facts?
- adopt an inferential rather than an expository style of teaching (see Table I, page 8)?
- surrounded and supported by oral work and by teacher explanation?
- provide opportunities for group work and discussion rather than isolating the pupil?
- reflect, whatever your subject, a responsibility for the language development of your pupils?
- assume value positions that you are not aware of?
- maintain a balance between writing, talking, listening and reading?
- take alternative approaches into account and not subject your pupils to 'death by a thousand worksheets'?

Variety

- direct pupils to locations other than their own desks?
- require pupils to use a variety of sources and resources?
- provide or support a variety of learning situations such as simulations, games, discussion, practical work, group work?
- offer the pupils a choice of activity or topic and allow them, at times, to follow their own interests?
- ask for a variety of response – oral, written, graphic, observation, making something?
- provide opportunities for written work to address a variety of audiences?

Construction

- cater for the needs of all levels of ability in the class?
- provide a properly ordered learning sequence in steps that are of a size appropriate to the age, ability and aptitudes of all your pupils?
- include procedures for diagnosis and remediation?
- provide sufficiently extending activities for the most able, e.g. problem solving, applying skills and concepts in different contexts, extended writing?
- avoid mindless blank filling and provide opportunities for processing information?
- give adequate information and clear, unambiguous instructions?
- avoid playing the 'what's in the teacher's mind' game?
- contain built-in check points at which every pupil will receive feedback from you?

Organization and management

- clearly labelled and coded for easy storage and retrieval?
- designed to be self-operating to ease problems of classroom management?
- backed up by well-ordered systems of recording progress and quick-marking systems for tests?

Needs of the slow learner

- Use material that is within or close to the child's experience?
- introduce new concepts in familiar contexts or settings?
- before asking a pupil for a piece of formal/transactional writing, allow opportunities for talk and for expressive writing?
- allow opportunities for making notes, drafting and redrafting before the final version?
- written in language that is easily understood?
- highlight and explain new words?
- use short sentences and simple sentence structures?
- avoid ambiguous words?
- refer only to other written materials that are within the pupil's reading ability?
- provide plenty of clues, cues, examples and opportunities for repetition and reinforcement?
- use small learning steps?
- give plenty of opportunities for success?
- typed and not handwritten?
- use large print that is compatible in size with the pupil's own handwriting?
- contain not more than ten words to the line?
- give only one teaching/learning point to the page?

- use a simple, uncluttered layout?
- contain plenty of illustrations?
- clearly differentiate between text and instructions, assignments etc.?
- in agreement with what the Remedial Specialist in your school thinks is appropriate for these children?

Visual quality

- make use of all the possibilities for presenting information visually rather than in written form, e.g. cartoon, flow-chart, tabular form, diagram?
- avoid too large an area of unrelieved print?
- make use of double and triple columns of text?
- use horizontal and vertical layouts to assist meaning and structure?
- have wide margins and make positive use of 'white space', e.g. space round illustrations, wider spacing between lines where key points are listed, space rather than lines on forms, tables etc.?
- have visually pleasing proportions between text, illustrations and white space?
- have continuity and compatability of styles of lettering?
- employ frames and boxes – around the whole worksheet, around diagrams and maps, to separate text from instructions?
- make use of the many aids for the non-artistic, e.g. tracings, dry transfer, copyright-free books?
- avoid excessive numbering of points, paragraphs etc.?
- have clearly captioned illustrations which are on the same page or adjacent to the relevant text?
- have a series of illustrations rather than all the information crammed into one picture?

Evaluation

- the result of consultation with colleagues and 'two heads rather than one'?
- operate within a system that allows for evaluation, improvement, change and updating?

Some helpful books

Long bibliographies tend to be rather depressing, so here is a short reading list to supplement and expand on some of the points made in this book:

Beach, M., *Editing your Newsletter*, Van Nostrand Reinhold, 1983

Beavis, R. & Weatherley, C., *Worksheets and School Learning*, SCET, 1980

Beswick, N., *Organizing Resources*, Heinemann Educational Books, 1975

Crabb, G., *Copyright Clearance: A Practical Guide*, CET, 1976

Davis, I.K., *The Management of Learning*, McGraw Hill, 1971

Eraut, M., Good, L. & Smith, G., *The Analysis of Curriculum Materials*, University of Sussex Occasional Paper 2, 1975

Hartley, J. & Burnhill, P., *Textbook Design: A Practical Guide*, Unesco, 1976

Hanson, J., *The Use of Resources*, Unwin Educational Books, 1975

Jenkins, J., Jones, G. & Lewis, R., *How to Write a Distance Learning Course* (11 units), CET, 1980

Laing, J. (ed.), *Do it Yourself Graphic Design*, Ebury Press, 1984

Lloyd-Jones, R. & Bray, E. (eds.), *Assessment: From Principles to Action*, Macmillan, 1985

Turke Kirkman, C., *Effective Writing: Improving Scientific, Technical and Business Communication*, E. & F.N. Spon, 1982

Zeitlyn, J., *Print: How you can do it Yourself*, Interaction Imprint, 1980

Index